SECRETS OF BREAK-THROUGH LEADERSHIP

By
Peter Capezio
and Debra Morehouse

CAREER PRESS
3 Tice Road
P.O. Box 687
Franklin Lakes, NJ 07417
1-800-CAREER-1
201-848-0310 (NJ and outside U.S.)
FAX: 201-848-1727

Secrets of Breakthrough Leadership

ISBN 1-56414-292-2, $16.99

Cover design by Foster & Foster

Printed in the U.S.A. by Book-mart Press

To order this title by mail, please include price as noted above, $2.50
handling per order, and $1.50 for each book ordered. Send to: Career
Press, Inc., 3 Tice Road., P.O. Box 687, Franklin Lakes, NJ 07417.

Or call toll-free 1-800-CAREER-1 (NJ and Canada: 201-848-0310) to
order using VISA or MasterCard, or for further information on books
from Career Press.

Library of Congress Cataloging-in-Publication Data

Capezio, Peter, 1947-
   Secrets of breakthrough leadership / by Peter Capezio and Debra
Morehouse.
     p. cm.
   Rev. ed. of: Taking aim on leadership. c1996
   Includes bibliographical references and index.
   ISBN 1-56414-292-2
   1. Leadership.   I. Morehouse, Debra L. II. Capezio, Peter, 1947-
Taking aim on leadership. III. Title.
HD57.7.C365 1997
658.4'092--dc21

                                                         97-7918
                                                          CIP

Legend Symbol Guide

Exercises that reinforce your learning experience.

Questions that will help you apply the critical points to your situation.

Checklist that will help you identify important issues for future application.

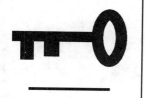

Key issues to learn and understand for future application.

CASE STUDY

Real-world case studies that will help you apply the information you've learned.

Table of Contents

Introduction

Increased competition in the global marketplace and rapid technological advancements have pushed for the need for leadership throughout every organization. That is the real intent behind "flattening" in organizations — to diminish management layers and place appropriate decision-making and responsiveness where it matters most — with the people doing the work. The alarm has sounded in corporate corridors and on the manufacturing floors throughout the U.S. — every job counts. Workers must add value to their companies, or they will put their companies and themselves out of business.

Speed-to-market requirements are demanding that workers and work groups solve problems quickly, make flexible adjustments and respond to customers dependably. Unprecedented market forces require radical changes in how companies work together on the inside. In order to achieve high-performance results, today's progressive companies are developing and training both management and the workforce for self-directed leadership — where everyone is a leader.

Self-directed leadership gives people the license to solve problems in their jobs. Companies used to expect their executives and managers to solve all the problems and make key decisions without the benefit of relying on worker experience. Today, problem-solving is no longer a top-down process. Good problem-solving requires that people throughout the organization learn effective leadership skills. This book will help you develop a mindset and the "know-how" you need to lead — **act, influence and motivate** — from anywhere in your organization.

Definition of Leadership

Leadership is the ability to influence individuals or groups to think, feel and take positive action to achieve goals.

Leading is the energizing component of management. In the past, leadership was viewed as "direction from the top" — where a vision of a future ideal state was revealed, the playing field was defined and the challenge to achieve goals was set into motion. Then, the management of a company assumed sole responsibility for assuring results.

Work is not done at the top, however. Today, companies are more concerned with the kind of leadership it takes to make great products, deliver outstanding service, cut costs and gain additional satisfied customers. This kind of leadership comes from a wellspring of talent and commitment among workers close to the customer and to the work. We call this kind of leadership self-directed.

Self-directed leadership challenges every team member — regardless of level — to help solve problems, improve quality, increase market share and create the kind of work environment that encourages people to do their best. You will recognize these kinds of companies because leadership is obvious. Top management sets the pace, and individuals and groups make decisions and take action deliberately and independently. If you work in such a company now, you know the meaning of what Nike projects in their statement, "Just Do It!"

> *"You cannot be a leader and ask other people to follow you, unless you know how to follow, too."*
> Sam Rayburn

Secrets of Breakthrough Leadership presents a model for self-directed leadership useful in leading yourself, your group and your organization. Self-directed leadership is based on your ability to understand and utilize the three core components of the AIM Leadership Model:

- **Action** — The ability to initiate strategy and change that serve as a catalyst around which others can align their efforts and together produce results that meet or exceed organizational, individual and team goals. Action creates results that reflect a company's vision, values and business and market strategy. Each action encourages a new action in others. Leadership strives for leveraging all positive actions together.

- **Influence** — The ability to cause others to willingly take a course of action and accept responsibility to pursue an outcome you desire. The power to influence others is at its best when listening and responsiveness to individual and group needs combine to produce actions which achieve goals. These goals benefit the business, the organization and its members.

- **Motivation** — The ability to harness one's own drive and succeed at having individual needs met in step with achieving organizational and group goals. Motivation comes both from within yourself and from outside sources, as people inspire thought and ignite their work environment. This support encourages everyone's best contributions. Leadership and followership change hands easily, and the focus is always on "How good can it be?"

The AIM Leadership Model will help you expand your understanding and effectiveness as a leader in your organization. It will help you become more self-confident and skilled in taking a leadership role, whether you are formally responsible for leading a division, work group or team. It will help you even if you are using informal ways to lead and influence team members, people in other parts of the company or your boss.

Self-directed leadership has come full cycle from where early theories of leadership began. The skills of effective leadership are not only now known to be learnable, but today's companies expect all people to lead in ways that matter most to product and process quality, company success and customer satisfaction. Leading is looked at as a servicing role. No longer do leaders chart the course for others without first listening to their followers, their leaders and other contributors. Self-directed leadership is self-responsibility for leading and following the right decisions for the right reasons.

Direction setting becomes a matter of group intelligence related to the experience of the marketplace and the company's technical capability to respond best to customer needs. Self-directed leaders learn how to listen and respond to the needs of others both within and outside the company. Self-directed leaders learn how to build alliances with others in a mutually sustaining process of action, influence and motivation. Finding the focus of this process is critical.

Leadership vs. Management

Management is keen on *doing* things right. Leadership is more concerned with doing the *right* things. There is a major distinction between thinking and acting as a manager and as a leader. The complex and creative work of individuals in companies today requires people to learn *both* management and leadership skills. The more competitive the marketplace, the more strategic and "on purpose" work behavior needs to be.

Leadership demands initiative and calculated risk-taking to try new ideas and to think and work differently than ever before. Management must deliver ongoing "best practices" to assure quality and customer satisfaction. Leadership depends on self-confidence and using one's sixth sense to link industry and business experience with the marketplace needs of the future. Management depends on control and accountability for today's performance. Leadership relies on creativity and responsibility for the future.

Companies and individuals need to develop *both* leadership and management capabilities and become adept at assessing when and how to use them. Historically, U.S. business schools have developed people to excel in the strategic and efficient management of capital to deliver higher rates of return. But there is a recent and dramatic turn in what both business schools and companies are expecting in management-development programs. Leadership is the key new ingredient.

> *"Leadership has a harder job to do than just choose sides. It must bring sides together."*
> Jesse Jackson

Later in this chapter, there is a grid contrasting leadership and management according to the corporate research of Harvard's John Kotter. Management capabilities focus on the hard science and core skills required to implement business decisions. Leadership draws its strength from developing a compelling rationale for *why* businesses should act in certain ways. Leadership focuses on vision and values and inspires people to believe and commit themselves to achieve goals.

Review the following descriptions of management and leadership and develop your own working definitions. Identify specific behaviors and skills you may need to expand your capabilities as an effective manager and leader.

Leadership

We must repeatedly ask the basic leadership question:

"Are we doing the right things?"

In its simplest form, leadership may be thought of as continually asking that single question. Leaders take the responsibility and **action** to **influence** and **motivate** a process of investigation that keeps everyone throughout the company buzzing to find out the answers to the question, "Are we doing the right things?" The "right things" about which leaders should be concerned address two core components:

1. **Business, Market and Customer Strategy** — Your "AIM" is on developing practices that add value to the products and services which respond to the needs of customers and make the company an industry leader. Leadership's job here is to provide:
   - Vision and mission
   - Direction

   that build a *strategic* purpose coupled with a sense of *urgency* to act.

2. **Organization Empowerment** — The focus is on creating a daily working environment where employees establish and outperform their own standards. Business strategy and expectations align with goals. Workers participate in all critical processes and make daily decisions which impact directly on the company's success. Participation, commitment

4

and self-directed leadership are the norm. Leadership's "job" here is to:

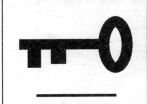

- *Share* the role of creating and nurturing the company's *culture*
- *Shape* and embrace the company's *core values* and
- *Unleash* its potential to create work processes and systems that produce desired results by developing people to manage change and transitions.

Keep focused on these two core components as you go through the **AIM Leadership Model.** You will be discovering ways to put these critical elements of leadership into practice and gain the respect and support of your co-workers. The **AIM Leadership Model** supports you in making a difference. This self-directed leadership difference will:

- *Impact* the kind and quality of the products and services the company delivers
- *Determine* how satisfied the customers are with the results
- *Guarantee* that you and the company are achieving results that keep you both out in front.

Leadership is both art and science. It is disciplined, creative and propelling. Leadership underlines our relationship with work, our customers and other members of the organization. Leadership at all levels in all people is about taking responsibility for results. Leadership is required in strategy, planning, work processing and evaluation. Leadership initiative throughout the organization is not a choice but a requirement for companies to be successful. Remember, the practice of leadership everywhere in the organization keeps focused on the question, "Are we doing the *right* things?"

1

Management

Management, on the other hand, has assumed the responsibility for "doing things right." For decades, business people have focused on how to perfect the key functions of management: planning, organizing, staffing, directing and controlling. These activities were clustered among managers who were given the formal power to direct the work of others. Over the past 100 years, management practices reflect our changing and emerging view of what we believe people are capable of.

Frederick Taylor's Scientific Management

Frederick Taylor, an early 20th-century productivity expert, influenced the organization of the U.S. manufacturing management system and dictated how work has been organized for much of this century. The management system was a rationale constructed to meet the unprecedented needs of a vast consumer market. It was based on Taylor's views of how he thought people needed to be managed and featured:

- hierarchical structure
- a formal chain of command
- position authority
- specialized functional departments
- job descriptions and responsibilities
- clear procedures and tracking systems

It was management's responsibility to harness technical and human resources to produce high volume. Managers and supervisors directed and controlled both work and workers.

Scientific-management theory reflects **Douglas McGregor's Theory X,** which basically views human beings as resistant to work and more responsive to clear direction and control. Taylor based his theories on physical science and thought that the "man most capable of doing the work was incapable of understanding the organization of the work." He thought, therefore, workers could not develop "general laws or rules" to reflect the science of work. Taylor saw clear divisions in *natural* ability among workers and managers. McGregor's *Theory X* person avoids responsibility, performs only under threat of punishment and wants security above all.

> *"We have, I fear, confused power with greatness."*
> Stewart Udall

Modern Management

Perfecting mass-production operations demanded a well-greased management system that reflected hierarchical structure and authority as well as functional departments that produced specific parts of the whole. Today, work teams typically are more engaged in producing the whole and do not require the control and monitoring of Taylor's scientific-management structure. Rather, today's operations require creative and fast-moving processes that integrate organizational resources quickly.

Modern management reflects **McGregor's Theory Y** where a person is viewed to have a *natural* capacity to expend both physical and mental ability at work and play. *Theory Y* people exercise self-direction and self-control and can produce organizational results when they are committed to the goals and if the rewards support their achievements. *Theory Y* people are creative and energetic, seek responsibility and frequently go unchallenged in bureaucratic and hierarchical organizations. *Theory Y* people are in high demand today. The principles of *Theory Y* form the base for self-directed leadership and point toward what is required in the development of the new workers.

Kotter's Management and Leadership Model

Harvard Business School's John Kotter has earned high marks from business people for his research and pragmatic models contrasting leadership with management. In the late 1980s, Kotter researched the experience of 200 executives in 11 U.S. corporations: American Express, ARCO, ConAgra, Digital Equipment Corporation, Kentucky Fried Chicken, Eastman Kodak, Mary Kay Cosmetics, NCR, Pepsi-Cola, Procter & Gamble and SAS.

Kotter's research included both personal interviews and written assessments and reports where people told of their experiences witnessing successful management and leadership practices in their organizations. They were asked how they believed management and leadership differed. They were asked to identify key behaviors — what people actually did — that constituted both "highly

> *"In our country, leadership has to establish itself. It is not taken for granted. It is not the inherent right of any caste. It does not proceed from generation to generation. It must prove itself."*
> Erwin D. Canham

7

> *"A competitive world has two possibilities for you. You can lose. Or, if you want to win, you can change."*
> Lester C. Thurow

effective management" and "highly effective leadership." Finally, participants were asked to identify what their companies needed from both in order to prosper over the next decade. The chart "Comparing Management and Leadership" summarizes the findings.

Kotter's research has helped to define the distinctly different behaviors of management and leadership. Reports and assessments from the companies Kotter interviewed provide an operational view of what leadership and management each contribute to the functioning of organizations. Kotter's research adds significantly to our understanding of the leadership dimension of work as something beyond charisma.

One of Kotter's key findings is that companies in the 80s were over-managed and underled. Companies frequently got lost managing systems without real insight about leading the industry or the people who delivered the results. A lot of dollars were spent on training and development without a clear understanding of the overall competencies required for marketplace success. Companies competing in a global economy with rapid change in markets and technology need to develop standards for both management and leadership. Deploying leadership incentives and management rationale and know-how among people at all levels of the organization are essential for the development, growth and continued success of companies.

Kotter's Management and Leadership Grid

	Management	Leadership
Creating an agenda	Planning and Budgeting — establishing detailed steps and timetables for achieving needed results and then allocating the resources necessary to make that happen.	Establishing Direction — a vision of the future, often the distant future, and strategies for producing the changes needed to achieve that vision.
Developing a human network for achieving the agenda	Organizing and Staffing — establishing some structure for accomplishing plan requirements, staffing that structure with individuals, delegating responsibility and authority for carrying out the plan, providing policies and procedures to help guide people and creating methods or systems to monitor implementation.	Aligning People — communicating the direction by words and deeds to all those whose cooperation may be needed so as to influence the creation of teams and coalitions that understand the vision and strategies and accept their validity.
Execution	Controlling and Problem-Solving — monitoring results vs. plan in some detail, identifying deviations and then planning and organizing to solve these problems.	Motivating and Inspiring — energizing people to overcome major political, bureaucratic and resource barriers to change by satisfying very basic, but often unfulfilled, human needs.
Outcomes	Produces a degree of predictability and order and has the potential of consistently producing key results expected by various stake-holders (e.g., for customers, always being on time; for stockholders, being on budget).	Produces change, often to a dramatic degree, and has the potential of producing extremely useful change (e.g., new products that customers want, new approaches to labor relations that help make a firm more competitive).

Reprinted with the permission of The Free Press, a Division of Simon & Schuster, Inc. from *A Force for Change: How Leadership Differs from Management* by John P. Kotter. Copyright 1990 by John P. Kotter, Inc.

Your Working Definitions of Leadership and Management

Draft your own working definitions of both management and leadership as they apply to you in your work.

Leadership is ..._____
_____

Management is ..._____
_____

List some capabilities you would like to enhance related to both management and leadership. Your work throughout this chapter will help you clarify and add to this initial list.

Leadership Capabilities

1. _____
_____
2. _____
_____
3. _____
_____
4. _____
_____
5. _____
_____

Management Capabilities

1. _____
_____
2. _____
_____
3. _____
_____
4. _____
_____
5. _____
_____

Shifting the Focus to Strong Leadership

Over the past century, U.S. industry has been much more focused on strong management. Companies that emphasize a more traditional management approach are characterized by:

- Planning and Budgets
- Policies and Procedures
- Controls and Monitoring
- Predictability and Stability

Although many of these companies experienced success in relatively stable economies, today's rapidly changing marketplace requires more emphasis on the bigger picture. Companies need to respond to changes in customer needs, competitive products and advances in technology. A shift is required, with more emphasis on strong leadership. Strong leadership is characterized by:

- Vision and Strategies
- Motivation and Inspiration
- Transition and Positive Change
- Satisfied Customers

Consider the desired path of strengthening leadership focus in your organization.

1. *What changes do you think need to occur?*

   _____

   _____

2. *What is necessary to increase your leadership mindset and capabilities?*

   _____

   _____

Shifting the Focus to Strong Leadership

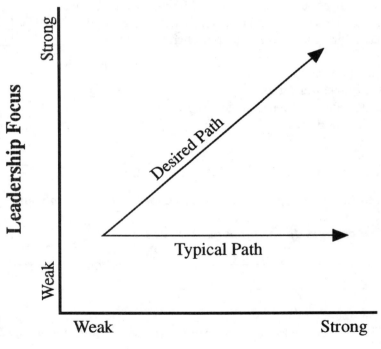

Acting from a Management and a Leadership Mindset

Consider these statements about work, and indicate which ones best reflect your viewpoint. Circle **a** or **b** in each group. Then review the key to determine how often you responded from a management or a leadership mindset. The key will also indicate which area of responsibility is being highlighted in each of the 10 examples.

There is no right or wrong approach. In actual practice, different situations require different responses. Good judgment and flexibility are essential in the new workplace. This exercise will demonstrate your fundamental beliefs and values regarding work and the capacity of workers to act independently from management. It will reveal your *predisposition* to think and act more from either a management or a leadership mindset. In actual practice, you need to develop both management and leadership capabilities.

1. a. Clear job descriptions are needed in today's complex business environment so people know what is expected of them.
    b. Today's business environment requires workers to "trouble shoot" their own jobs and determine what past expectations and functions are becoming obsolete.

2. a. Workers need their managers to set performance goals and then allow them to figure out how best to accomplish their own work.
    b. Workers need clear direction from their supervisors about how to do their jobs.

3. a. Managers need to understand business information such as marketplace performance, the need for new products and what the competition is doing, while workers have little need to know.

   b. Workers need a continuous connection between the impact of their work and how well the company is doing regarding market response, competitor positioning and projections of future strategy and product development.

4. a. Planning is the domain of top management, where the goals of a company and each business need to be spelled out clearly for managers, supervisors and employees. Communication and planning flow top-to-bottom.

   b. Top management is ultimately accountable for the future direction and planning of a company and its businesses. However, all members of an organization (including *external* constituents such as suppliers, customers and competitors) have valuable experiences and input for creating the future direction of an organization. Communication and planning flow outside-in, bottom-to-top and then top-to-bottom.

5. a. The chain of command provides clear lines of authority and security for managers and workers. It creates an essential and expedient organization of work for today's modern business environments. All people understand who is responsible for what and who has the authority to make certain kinds of decisions.

   b. Today's competitive marketplace requires a breakdown and dramatic restructuring of organizations where past bureaucratic hierarchies, the chain of command, functional "silo" departments and formal position authority are impediments to making decisions and doing the best for the customer.

6. a. Individual, professional development is recognized as a key motivation for employee commitment to the company. The companies who are surviving and excelling in the competitive global marketplace are committed to training and developing their people for high performance both now and in the future. These companies are succeeding because they know their employees are the real "brain trust" of their businesses.

b. Today's companies no longer need the long-term commitment of their workforce because rapid change demands new skills. Labor is now viewed as disposable and available on demand in the society at large to supply future needs.

7. a. Promotions should be infrequent and replaced with frequent job rotations to broaden employees so they gain a breadth of understanding about the business. Natural curiosity, adaptability and a broad range of interpersonal skills are the most important criteria for top managers and leaders.

b. Promotions should be frequent and based on an employee's outstanding performance in a current position and functional area. The single most important criteria for top managers and leaders is their specialized, technical expertise. Past performance is the best indicator of how well they will do in the future.

8. a. Workers look to team leaders to solve problems and settle work-group disputes in advance by providing rules for team functioning and clear assignments to each team member.

b. Team leaders facilitate and coach team members to organize the work of the team, establish team goals, make unique contributions, lead and follow one another and solve problems together as they arise.

9. a. Performance is best evaluated by supervisors and managers who establish performance expectations and provide resources and direction for workers to excel. Feedback is documented during annual performance appraisals and responds to goals that were established in advance by the supervisor or manager.

b. Performance is best evaluated through a fluid process which engages the individual, his boss, other co-workers and even customers — who all help to shape performance expectations in the first place. Feedback is continuous and relevant to goals and new expectations which take shape and are reestablished between a worker and his boss.

10. a.   Incentives for team performance should include recognition for individual contributions based on expectations that the team establishes and revises along with the team leader. Decisions about individual contributions should be made among the peer group with input from the team leader.

b.   Incentives for team performance should be constructed to emphasize individual contributions. The team leader is in the best position to evaluate individual contributions to diminish foul play and jealousy among peers.

Key to Exercise

The key below shows which **a** or **b** responses reflect a management and a leadership mindset. The key also shows the area of responsibility for each question. Remember both management and leadership responses are valid. Your judgment in when to apply a particular approach is what matters most. Management responses focus on "doing things right"; leadership focuses on "doing the right things."

Example	Manager	Leader	Area of Responsibility
1	a	b	Organizing work, job descriptions, "what" is expected
2	b	a	Setting performance goals, initiative to decide "how" work is done
3	a	b	Sharing information about the business, "need to know"
4	a	b	Planning, direction of information and communication
5	a	b	Structuring work and the organization, authority and decision-making
6	b	a	Staffing, employee development and training, partnering
7	b	a	Staffing, employee development and training, promoting
8	a	b	Directing, team roles and team functioning
9	a	b	Controlling, setting individual performance expectations, measuring individual performance
10	b	a	Controlling, setting team-performance expectations, measuring individual and team contributions

Increasing Your Leadership Mindset Exercise

Shift from a Management to a Leadership Mindset

Review the following contrasts representing a shift from a management to a leadership mindset. Identify instances when you might make decisions based upon each *shift* in mindset.

THINKING/PLANNING

From *Management:* **Tactical Concentration**

Management focuses its lens on applications and tactical concerns. Thinking centers on the question, "How do things actually work?"

To *Leadership:* **Strategic Direction**

Leadership requires one to have a keen navigational sense to guide the direction of where the work is going. The key questions here relate to asking, "What does the marketplace need?" and, "How can we best provide it according to our capabilities and resources?"

_____

_____

_____

GOAL-SETTING

From *Management:* **Past Performance**

Management focuses on goal-setting by making projections of future success based on past performance. By evaluating past customer response and making certain assumptions about the future, the management mindset is asking, "How can we increase our market share?"

To *Leadership:* **Future Impact**

Leadership approaches goal-setting by anticipating future market trends and then determining what strengths the company possesses in order to respond in new and creative ways. Questions focus on, "How can we take our core capabilities and respond to changing market conditions?"

_____

_____

_____

LEVERAGING

From *Management:* **Current Operations**

Management examines the efficiency and effectiveness of how a company and its components have organized the work. Acting in a management mindset requires one to troubleshoot current practices and work methods and ask, "Is this the best way to do them?"

To *Leadership:* **Future Impact**

Leadership anticipates future needs and communicates incentives to the organization and its members for change and transition. Peering into the future, a leadership sense asks, "What trends will evolve and how can we position ourselves to be there first and fast?"

USING POWER

From *Management:* **Control**

Management is responsible to develop reliable reportage mechanisms for controlling the operations of a company. Management must always be in a dependable and informed position to answer such pragmatic questions as, "How much? How often? At what cost?"

To *Leadership:* **Influence**

Leadership requires one to explore "outside the box" and to influence others to do the same. It is the opposite of control, which is geared to hang on to power. Positive influence is empowering others. Inventiveness, a spirit of adventure and an ability to "color outside the lines" are useful attributes that set the stage for discovering the new and unfamiliar. Here, a leadership perspective is asking, "What if we didn't always do things this way?"

ORGANIZING

From *Management:* **Segmentation/Parts**

Management prompts recognition of the various components of the whole — an identification of the many, specific parts. The focus is on determining the right divisions, functional areas and job classifications. Management oversees responses to such questions as, "Who is responsible for this? Where is this procedure done?"

To *Leadership:* **Integration/The Whole**

Leadership is intent on understanding relationships of the parts to the whole. Focus is on the ability of the company to combine its strengths and resources optimally in serving its customers. Leadership asks such questions as, "Why is this a separate unit? What benefit is achieved by duplication? How can the customer receive better follow-through from sale to service?"

IMPLEMENTING

From *Management:* **Systems**

Management is fixed on developing responsive systems, those which can flex to the needs of the customers and still provide the essential control required to track the business. Management is very committed to asking such things as, "What can we do to improve this system? What will we gain from this technology? Should we make it or buy it?"

To *Leadership:* **Processes**

Leadership examines how the work is done. It is committed to improving processes and assuring expedient interfaces among all those involved with product and service development and delivery. Leadership is probing linkages and results in work flow with such questions as, "Why do you do it this way? Where does your work come from? What do you contribute? Who benefits from your work? Where does it go next?"

PERFORMING/CONTRIBUTING AS AN INDIVIDUAL
From *Management:* **Individual Performance**

Management develops job focus and job descriptions which highlight position responsibilities and direct people to meet specific expectations. Management addresses such questions as, "How prepared are you to fulfill this requirement? Given the gap that exists between job expectations and your skill base, what training and development is required? How can we best measure your progress?"

To *Leadership:* **Individual Contribution**

Leadership assumes the role of inspiring individuals to contribute unique strengths that may not be specified in the job description or be part of an official performance appraisal. Leadership asks, "What is unique about this individual worker? Can these strengths benefit the organization? What will it cost the organization to unleash this talent? How can we encourage and reward this individual for this output?"

_____

_____

_____

PERFORMING/CONTRIBUTING AS A WORK GROUP OR TEAM
From *Management:* **Work-Group Performance**

Management assigns tasks and monitors the results of work groups to assure the most beneficial work-group performance. There is a watchful eye to compare the results of a work group in contrast with the effectiveness of individuals working separately. Management is concerned with the answers to questions like, "How long did it take you? Did the input of others in the group help you accomplish the work in a more efficient or improved way?"

To *Leadership:* **Team Contribution**

Leadership focuses on cross-divisional, cross-functional and problem-solving teams whose members come from throughout the company. Teams are looked to for innovation and breaking through a company's traditional ways of working. A leadership lens views team output for its value related to such tasks as reducing cycle times, creating more harmony within the company and reducing internal divisional competition. Leadership asks, "Have we gained speed-to-market in this new cross-functional, product development process? Will we gain more fairness throughout the company with this cross-divisional compensation policy? Will this new policy encourage broad-based career development?"

_____

_____

_____

COMMUNICATING
From *Management:* **Top–Down Communication**

Management tradition has depended on top-down communication where each layer of management has been informed by the previous one as to the dictates of the top leadership. Chain of command, protocol, formality and prescribed ways of responding all characterized this type of communication. While there are many modifications to this traditional communication pattern, a management mindset is still very invested in assuring that leadership's message is delivered to and understood by those employees within their own span of control. Management asks, "Is there a full understanding of how to apply the new safety procedures? Do you understand the company's new customer strategy in this product line? Do you agree with the new compensation package?"

To *Leadership:* **Multi–Directional Communication**

Leadership views communication as multi-directional — top-down, bottom-up and criss-crossed throughout the organization. Leadership views people as linking pins in their various roles, responsible for empowering one another with information. They challenge practices when their own insights may provide a new view. Leadership questions relate to such things as, "Have you integrated the guidelines that the XYZ Division developed last year? Are you using the benchmarking data from the research group? Have you all contributed your input to the memo our division is forwarding to the CEO? Are you having any problems with the company's new 360° feedback process?"

PROBLEM-SOLVING

From *Management:* **Solving Problems**

Management takes the task approach to solving problems. Historically, management has been chartered to solve problems. Top leadership and workers alike looked toward those in management to know what was going on and how to fix anything that wasn't working. Today's management mindset may still be directing team members to solve problems but with the emphasis on *solve* and less on the problem itself. Management questions focus on, "How long will it take you? How much will it cost? Who else needs to be involved?"

To *Leadership:* **Asking Questions**

Leadership initiative is committed to "solving the problem" as well, but gives full weight to taking the time to identify and understand what problem needs to be solved. Typically, managers and workers are so intent on solving the problem that the energy is almost totally placed in "fixing things." A leadership perspective probes the situation and asks unusual questions that may help uncover root causes or true problems. They ask such questions as, "Why did that occur then? Who else worked on this? What is the missing piece? Where did the communication break down? Who issued the specifications? How were change orders recorded?"

_____

_____

_____

INFLUENCING

From *Management:* **Directing/Assessing**

Management gives the responsibility of clarifying the work-output needs of the company to the workers and then assessing their performance against those expectations. Management relies on providing clear direction and measuring performance in ways that inform workers and the company of progress being made on achieving both individual and company goals. Management provides direction and assessment in such ways as, "The goal is to reduce costs by 15 percent, and that means you can make recommendations in your own areas for these cuts. You need to have the policy manual completed by the beginning of the third quarter; develop an action plan and schedule for review within the next week. Your position has expanded to include responsibility for project management; we have scheduled a three-week training program for you next month."

To *Leadership:* **Coaching/Empowering**

Leadership views its role as one of "coach" and mentor which empowers colleagues and co-workers to set work standards and achievement goals. These objectives are in step with the company and push it further toward a new horizon. A leadership mindset is one keen on "raising the bar" by energizing the environment to unleash its talent. Leadership coaching and empowering sound like, "What can you make of the company's goals for next year? How can your work contribute to these aspirations? What else can you think of to sharpen the company's focus? Do you have enough information and knowledge of company resources to develop your own work plan for next year? How will you link rewards to achievements in your work plan?"

_____

_____

_____

LEADERSHIP STYLES

Effective leaders gain insight into themselves and others and develop flexible styles that get results in different situations. Individuals require varying amounts of direction, support and recognition. Leaders who want to optimize the contributions of each worker will respond appropriately with a leadership style that works well for each person.

There are four leadership styles which have developed around the use of authority. These styles have different impacts on individuals with varying needs for direction, support and recognition from a leader:

- **Autocratic Leadership** — An autocratic leader operates as one who commands and expects compliance, who is dogmatic and leads by the ability to give or withhold rewards and punishment. This type of leadership aligns with McGregor's Theory X assumptions of human nature. Autocratic leaders played a large role in Taylor's scientific management and are now becoming obsolete in progressive companies structured to encourage self-directed leadership among their members.

- **Democratic, Participative Leadership** — A democratic leader consults with members of the group on proposed actions and decisions and encourages and rewards participation. This type of leader acts along a continuum of response from the subordinates, including not acting without the approval of the group and acting with full participation. Leaders must make decisions and set direction. Democratic leaders will be respected more than autocratic leaders for an unpopular decision if they concur with members first and listen to the resistance among the group before taking action. Democratic, participative leaders will exemplify McGregor's *Theory Y* view of human nature. However, these leaders are adaptive and can be effective with followers who may be operating more from McGregor's *Theory X*.

- **Free-Rein Leadership** — A free-rein leader expects those they lead to operate with a high degree of autonomy and independence. These leaders exert their authority very little because of the readiness level of their group to set goals, develop strategy and harness themselves and the necessary resources to deliver results. Free-rein leaders see their role as one of assisting the operations of followers by obtaining relevant information for them, accessing remote resources, reducing organizational barriers and generally serving as an interface with the external environment. This type of leader fulfills the requirements of being a servant leader and is most effective with people who reflect McGregor's Theory Y assumptions about human nature.

- **Blended Leadership Style** — A leader who utilizes a blended leadership style is taking into account the specific conditions of the project or process, individual employees and their preparedness to succeed on the job. These leaders flex with the circumstances and adapt to the needs of their followers. They use a variety of behaviors including coaching, training, telling and demonstrating to promote optimum autonomy among workers while assuring the best results for the customer.

A Combination of Styles Is Needed in Today's Workplace

Autocratic   Democratic

Blended

Match Style
to Circumstance

Free-Rein

Many leaders react to very different circumstances with the same style of approach. The blended leadership style requires flexibility and a response which matches the style with the specific circumstances.

Preferred Leadership Style Assessment

Directions: Here are 12 sentences that describe leadership styles. Read each one and decide your degree of preference for each. Circle 1–5 indicating your strength of preference. When you are finished, score your answers to find out your preferred leadership style.

	Almost Never Prefer	Seldom Prefer	Some–times Prefer	Frequently Prefer	Almost Always Prefer
1. Leader sets direction without input from followers.	1	2	3	4	5
2. Leader sets direction and considers input from followers.	1	2	3	4	5
3. Leader and followers set direction together.	1	2	3	4	5
4. Leader sets direction based on instruction from followers.	1	2	3	4	5
5. Leader evaluates progress with little input from followers.	1	2	3	4	5
6. Leader and followers evaluate progress together.	1	2	3	4	5
7. Leader reverses decision without input from followers due to an emergency.	1	2	3	4	5
8. Leader evaluates progress based on followers' judgments.	1	2	3	4	5
9. Leader makes all decisions unilaterally.	1	2	3	4	5
10. Leader makes decisions with participation of followers.	1	2	3	4	5
11. Leader approves decisions of followers.	1	2	3	4	5
12. Leader abides by decisions of followers.	1	2	3	4	5

Leadership Style Scores: Total your points for each of the questions listed under the styles.

	Autocratic	Democratic/Participative	Free-Rein
Questions:	_____	_____	_____
	1,5,7,9 (add points)	2,3,6,10 (add points)	4,8,11,12 (add points)

The highest score will indicate your tendency in leadership style. However, if your score was balanced among the three styles, you probably have a tendency to use a blended style of leadership, which is based on the specific circumstances of the situation.

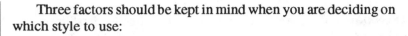

Deciding Which Leadership Style to Use

Three factors should be kept in mind when you are deciding on which style to use:

1. The individual or team involved
2. The circumstances involved
3. Your preferred leadership style

Considerations:

- The level of commitment and experience will cause you to apply a specific style.
- Time constraints may affect the style you are able to utilize.
- The appropriate leadership style for different members of the group may not match the leader's preferred style of leading. If there is a "mismatch," the leadership will not be as effective, and the workers will not perform at their best. Leaders learn to identify the needs of followers and to adapt their leadership styles to accommodate the needs of the group through increased awareness and training. Today's leaders who seek tomorrow's best performance are focused on encouraging self-directed leadership throughout the organization. Self-directed leadership unleashes the leader in each individual in the company.

Self-directed leadership underscores the **AIM Model of Leadership.** While it reflects all the styles just referenced, except the autocratic leadership style, it mostly resembles a free-rein leadership style. Self-directed leadership makes its distinction by focusing on the leadership capacity of individuals who do not formally direct the work of others, as well as leaders who do. The emphasis is on people assuming individual responsibility to assert leadership in areas where they have good ideas and a direct connection to the work. Self-directed leadership is not concerned with *formal authority*.

Self-directed teams, for example, are formed to challenge teams to initiate their own project development. Formal authority requires people to have prescriptions to influence or be influenced by others.

Self-management. Here the baton of team contributor and team leader flows easily from hand to hand as the demands of the project call upon the expertise of particular individuals. Formal authority in past U.S. structures reflected the notion of control which became synonymous with the concept of management.

People resist being managed because it reminds them of being controlled. People seek leadership because they are curious about the future and want to know the general direction of the company or work team so they can make a valued contribution. They will join in the effort if they perceive the goals to be worthwhile. John Kotter's work with U.S. companies of the 1980s found they were overmanaged and underled. There was too much control and not enough direction.

The turnaround companies in the 1990s and beyond are pushing to drive leadership throughout the organization. They want to equip people to become effective using both management and leadership skills. Companies who learn how to do that will succeed at influencing their people to:

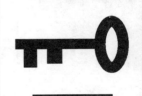

- **align behind a vision and mission**
- **establish organization, business, team and individual performance goals**
- **inspire, motivate and participate actively in a self-directed leadership culture**
- **seek innovation and invent new processes as well as products**
- **partner with people anywhere inside and outside the organization to solve problems and serve customers**
- **redefine the value and balance of their work and personal lives**

Self-directed leadership as reflected in the **AIM Model** will carry companies into the future. Examine the *Company Profile* to learn what one company is doing to develop self-directed leadership among their leaders.

Company Profile

AT&T's Leadership Development Program

For those of you who may doubt that the new wave of self-directed leadership is a requirement for the survival of forward-thinking companies, listen to what some of AT&T's managers are saying about their new leadership-development program.

"A leader has to know when to step back."

"It's hard to be a worker bee when you are used to being a manager."

"Managers struggle with holding back that creativity and continuing to control so people aren't growing."

"I wouldn't say we are there yet, but we are working on the redefinition of a leader from a controller to a coach."

"There are fewer promotions, but we are being broadened and developed to know more about the whole business than ever before. There is a different kind of satisfaction. It means we have to redefine the value we have placed on position levels and status."

"The fundamental nature of our contribution is shifting dramatically."

AT&T is learning that to be a global leader in the communications industry, they have to recognize the contributions that workers can make every day. Further, the company has to embrace the global diversity of both their customers and employees. Unleashing creativity and leadership within the company is an essential step to serving customers optimally. Not only is AT&T revamping how it trains its leaders, but it is doing so in such a way as to develop people in a cross-cultural context.

Forty middle managers in their thirties and forties from around the globe meet in a two-week program designed for "high potentials." At $4,000 per week a person, only 200 of the company's 28,000 middle managers have gone through the program each of the last several years. However, there is no question that the company's chairman, Bob Allen, holds this program as the model for developing AT&T's future leadership.

The program emphasis is on mentoring people to take risks and to act in a more entrepreneurial way. Just a few years ago, the Harvard case study method was used. Reliance on case studies only seemed to make managers better at doing their current jobs. Now, the program is focused on managing change and helps managers anticipate their jobs of tomorrow. Learning vehicles provide opportunities for managers to "think outside the boxes" and try new ideas and behaviors with their cohorts in an attempt to achieve greater worker participation.

AT&T is experiencing shifts in how managers are thinking and acting as a result of their development in the program. For example, people are solving customer problems by working with colleagues at the same level. They are creating and implementing solutions without referencing a "chain of command" hierarchy that has been the company's norm. The results indicate that problem-solving is more immediate and customer satisfaction is increasing.

Managers are realizing that promotions aren't as frequent, but they are gaining more breadth in their careers through AT&T's leadership-development initiatives. Also, there is a new norm emerging away from the AT&T 10-hour day, to a day which allows workers more balance between their work and personal lives. People who take a break from the job are now considered better able to perform while they are there.

AT&T has even revamped its mission in recent years. It used to see itself as a telephone company. Now, its mission is "to bring people together." No matter what it takes, the company will create and use technology to provide customers with greater access to one another in more time-efficient and cost-effective ways no matter how remote the locations. The management philosophy of the company is moving away from control, while aiming its future on leadership's ability to coach and mentor a self-directed work force. AT&T knows its ability to work collectively is a cornerstone to achieving the innovations it needs to remain the *global* industry leader.

The new challenge for leaders is to influence, motivate and inspire action among the members of an organization without relying on the old models of authority. This direction is especially courageous in an atmosphere where the paternalistic environment of job security has gone out the window. The **AIM Leadership Model,** which relies on **Action, Influence and Motivation,** aligns well with AT&T's leadership-development initiatives and centers on empowering people to lead without authority.

Forward-looking companies are making the commitment to develop people to make leadership contributions as part of the norm rather than the exception in the course of their daily work. Companies like AT&T are "raising the bar" on what is expected and are placing greater emphasis on the necessity of driving leadership throughout the organization.

Leadership-development programs need to reorient their challenge to workers and encourage:

- team participation
- independent thinking
- adaptability to change
- flexibility to shift from leading to following
- replacement of a "chain of command" structure with one that is organized around meeting customer needs
- balancing individual attention on both career and life goals

Personal Readiness to Lead Assessment

Evaluate your own *readiness* to lead by answering the following questions. Rate your behavior and your willingness to lead on a scale of 1–5. Higher numbers represent your increasing comfort and competence to assume leadership in particular ways.

Not Comfortable		Moderately Comfortable		Very Comfortable
1	2	3	4	5

1. I am generally knowledgeable about my company and our industry.

1	2	3	4	5

2. I seek out information on my own both inside and outside the company in order to stay current in my specific functional area.

1	2	3	4	5

3. I make it a practice to speak plainly with my boss about ideas and recommendations I have which may cause business to be conducted in a different manner.

1	2	3	4	5

4. I get a great deal of satisfaction out of working on assignments with little specific direction.

1	2	3	4	5

5. I find it fairly easy to understand people who are different from me.

1	2	3	4	5

6. I enjoy the opportunity to take on a challenging assignment where I get to coordinate the work efforts of my peers throughout the company.

   1   2   3   4   5

7. I pride myself in being able to adapt my work process and the results to accommodate my co-workers.

   1   2   3   4   5

8. I like being asked to serve on a cross-functional or cross-divisional team and learn more about how we can mutually strengthen our products and services or even create new ones.

   1   2   3   4   5

9. I am always planning for the next steps in my own professional development and examining how my goals match up with what the company needs.

   1   2   3   4   5

10. I take risks on the job by expressing my opinion, even if I think others won't like it. I routinely act "out of the norm" because I have a drive to seek improvements.

   1   2   3   4   5

If you have moderate or low comfort level on more than 50 percent of the questions, you should take advantage of the **Action, Influence and Motivation** chapters to help give you the tools to increase your readiness to be a leader in your organization.

Questions for Personal Development

1. What is the major emphasis of this chapter?

_____

_____

_____

_____

2. What are the most important things you learned from this chapter?

_____

_____

_____

_____

3. How can you apply what you learned to your current job?

_____

_____

_____

_____

4. How will you go about making these changes?

_____

_____

_____

_____

5. How can you monitor improvement?

_____

_____

_____

_____

6. Summarize the changes you expect to see in yourself one year from now.

_____

_____

_____

_____

CHAPTER 2

What Leaders Do

Leadership is the ability to influence individuals or groups to take positive action to achieve specific goals.

The **AIM Leadership Model** has been developed to focus on key steps you can take to enhance your ability to lead. You will find the model useful as you attempt to figure out what you need to do in various situations to reduce complexity and chaos.

In order to really understand what you need to do as a leader, ask a few basic questions:

What do people look for from leaders? And, specifically, what do people need from me? How can I contribute to maximize this opportunity for the company? How can I help each person give their best?

Here are 5 key points to follow in providing effective leadership:

1. Seek to understand whole situations
2. Respect and value different kinds of people
3. Determine what motivates each individual
4. Develop insight and good judgment
5. Adapt your leadership style to the situation and the individual

The **AIM Leadership Model** gears leaders to take **action, influence and motivate** their colleagues and subordinates to feel free to contribute and lead themselves. Here are four steps leaders can take to encourage others to make their best contributions:

1. Help individuals link the satisfaction of their own needs (professional and personal) with meeting company and customer expectations.
2. Set the example of give and take so people are comfortable both in leading and following.
3. Encourage new ideas and methods, and make sure the rewards are in the right place.
4. Support ongoing development and training.

Five Building Blocks of Effective Leadership

There are five building blocks upon which a leader develops skills in order to be effective. These five cornerstones form a foundation which underlines the **AIM Leadership Model — Action, Influence and Motivation**. You should note some of your own ideas about what leaders do and what skills they need to succeed as leaders.

1. COMMUNICATION

Leaders develop a variety of competencies related to effective communication. Listening, observing and providing feedback are some of a leader's most powerful tools. These skills are powerful because they provide leaders with a true bridge into understanding others and helping workers to understand themselves and their work situations.

Understanding is the key **which influences individuals or groups to take positive action to achieve specific goals** — the real essence of what leaders do. Good communication is the key to understanding. Understanding leads to insight and results in self-confidence. Self-confidence is essential for people to act on their own initiative. Good leaders know how to listen, understand and provide feedback to help others gain insight and self-confidence to act.

"Leadership should be born out of the understanding of the needs of those who would be affected by it."
Marian Anderson

2

Note: Guidelines for developing solid listening skills are outlined in Chapter 4.

Leaders also are distinguished by their ideas. Leaders need to be able to paint pictures that show people an *ideal* future state. People become inspired and motivated based upon the strength of a leader's ideas. The ideas can only come alive for people through communication. Our electronic age is making it possible for leaders to communicate in very expedient and dynamic ways. However, not even the best writers and multimedia wizards can capture the imagination of one's followers without first starting with a leader who has a compelling message.

Leaders are most effective for telling the simple truth. Leaders who can make the complex simple and can lead their division or work groups through complexity to achieve real results receive admiration and commitment from their people. Telling the appropriate amounts of the right kind of information speeds people in a focused direction that only makes the next steps closer. Leaders set an example of communication that will be replicated in a team, division or company. Efficient communication is direct, honest and comes in appropriate amounts.

> *"True leadership is the art of changing a group from what it is into what it ought to be."*
> Virginia Allan

2. DEVELOPING FOLLOWERS

Leaders know how to give away power and make others around them powerful. Leaders also learn how to dispense and pace this distribution of power. A leader must take time to know each person and their unique capacity to flourish. People move along at variable rates. Leaders set a pace in a company and establish expectations.

However, for people to join in the game, they need to be treated as individuals with special talents and gifts which need to be identified, assessed and developed further. Some of the discussion in Chapter 1 on leadership styles will be useful to you in thinking about your own orientation toward developing followers. Successful leaders grow successful followers and commit to transforming them into leaders who in turn pass leadership throughout the company. Leaders instill the ability to listen and respond to customer needs, especially as these needs drive future business.

3. FOCUS ON KEY ISSUES

Leaders develop a tenacity to stay focused on the key issues. They accomplish this through planning, goal-setting and tracking progress against an action plan. Customer needs change and create emerging niche markets. Leaders need to keep one eye squinting into the future to discover how tomorrow's work, structure and process might best serve those emerging markets.

Leaders take on the challenge of new learning themselves and expect it from those around them. Development and training become second nature in a culture where leadership is expected from all the players. Leaders know the future is invented by those who are not only yearning but learning and inventing new products, processes, resources and customer-delivery systems. Leaders focus daily on how to improve their work processes and reward those colleagues and subordinates who do the same.

Leaders develop a personal style of discipline which allows them enough structure to keep their attention and energy harnessed. Creativity needs some channeling so it can become accessible by others. Effective leaders realize as they solve today's problem, they don't want to create tomorrow's fire.

Leaders need to remain both focused and fluid. To achieve this, leaders become intimate with the daily operations of the business as well as how well it is performing in the marketplace. Leaders put into place mechanisms which give them instant access and familiarity with customers, competitors, vendors and colleagues both inside and outside the company.

Leaders must guarantee that they are on top of the business while at the same time anticipating where the business should go next. They need to know if customers are satisfied, how well a new product launch is going, if productivity has improved with increased technology or if the team is functioning near peak performance. They need to use current performance as a leverage to gain speed in the marketplace.

"The fine art of executive decision consists of not deciding questions that are not now pertinent, in not deciding prematurely, in not making decisions that cannot be made effective and in not making decisions that others should make."
Chester I. Barnard

2

4. LINK WITH OTHERS

Leaders keep vital by developing links both inside and outside their companies. Sharing ideas, experiences, information and resources tends to increase everyone's capacity and productivity. Networking becomes a necessity for being on the leading edge. In order for dreams to become reality, people "buy in" to leadership's vision. For the vision to stand a reality check, leaders need to cast a broad net in building links with others.

More than ever, links with people inside and outside the company are critical for business success. You may have experienced one or more restructurings in your own company within the last few years where people are clustered, not so much by functional areas, e.g., accounting, marketing, manufacturing, but more along product and customer lines. You may be operating on several teams and have certain responsibilities to a team leader for which you are accountable while, at the same time, you may also report to a unit or functional area head. Now, people on the inside of companies are working together in market-driven structures and processes.

Business-process reengineering revamps work processes to eliminate non-value added activity and redundancy. Total quality management strives to eliminate waste and achieve continuous improvement. The goal with both strategies is to put people in direct link with one another to expedite the flow of work.

External connections are equally important at all levels of the company. Benchmarking best practices with other companies can reveal pivotal information and experiences that can save your company time and money. Professional development frequently requires mentors, not only from within the company, but from the outside. The rate of technological advancements and emerging industry trends require continuous access to on-line information which parallels industry and customer experience.

> *"Leaders do not rest on their laurels for long if they expect to remain leaders. Initiative is a necessary quality for anyone who aspires to rise above the crowd clustered at the foot of the ladder of success; it is characteristic of all true leaders."*
> Boyd Lindop

2

5. PERSONAL AND PROFESSIONAL BALANCE

Individual leaders need to commit to balance in their own lives. This is easier said than done but ultimately is required for leaders to become models who inspire others to want to make similar commitments. When leaders achieve personal and professional balance, they bring a tone and quality to their work and decisions which earn their followers' trust, respect and a strong desire to practice the leader's own behavior or emulate their characteristics and qualities.

The keys to balance include: self-knowledge (values, interests, talents and priorities), truth, consideration for and inclusion of others and discipline to nourish all that is human in oneself and others — mind, body and spirit. There is no substitute for the resulting tone that balance creates in one's thinking, judgment and behavior. Personal and professional balance puts into practice the saying, "...keep your head when those all around you are losing theirs." In order for leaders to "keep their heads," they must understand and be dedicated to their own personal and professional development.

Challenging questions are arising related to the perception of contrasting levels of professional commitment among various age groups as measured by such values as willingness to work long hours, to relocate and to take on very difficult assignments. Perhaps younger managers are alerted to some imbalance in the personal and professional lifestyles they have perceived among their mentors and leaders. Is there not an emergent and unifying concern that personal and family happiness and well-being are under attack in western society — perhaps everywhere in the world? Is there not some critical mass of perception and alarm that our values are out of sync with such balance as one might determine as essential in living a satisfying life or leading a company or nation?

Coming to terms with personal and professional balance is a key issue as we move into the 21st century. Leaders who commit to solving some of the new millennium's challenges must realize their position in history and time and bring balance to their lives and leadership. Balance in mind, body and spirit. Commitment to the

> *"Nothing great will ever be achieved without great men, and men are great only if they are determined to be so."*
> Gen. Charles de Gaulle

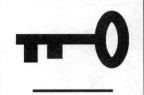

2

human in all of us. Not by technology alone will we move forward. Leadership must model the balance and tone we need for both discovery and preservation.

NOTE: Keep these five building blocks in mind as you explore and examine the three kinds of leaders we identify as necessary for moving leadership throughout the organization later in this chapter.

The Five Building Blocks of Effective Leadership

Style

Building Block	Autocratic	Democratic/Participative	Free-Rein	Blended
Communication	Mostly one way. Top down	Two-way. Interaction to get buy-in	Two-way. Follower-driven	Two-way. Both leader- and follower-initiated
Developing Followers	Conductor	Teacher	Coach	Mentor
Focus on Key Issues	Top-down agenda	Leader-initiated agenda	Follower-initiated agenda	Collaborative agenda
Link With Others	Hierarchical	Consensual	Creative	Flexible
Personal and Professional Balance	Self-contained	Interdependent	Diverse	Individualized

The chart illustrates how leadership styles utilize the five building blocks in day-to-day interactions. As you learn to apply the appropriate leadership styles, you should focus on how the impact of your building blocks enables you to become an effective leader.

2

COMPANY PROFILES

Putting the Five Building Blocks to Work

CYPRESS SEMICONDUCTOR

Cypress Semiconductor, a Silicon innovator, has pioneered a system of self-imposed goal-setting where employees update their own goals weekly every Monday morning. Coordinated through PC-based software, employees provide updates on previous goals and revise their plans from a week earlier, always focusing on what they will achieve over the next month and a half. By Wednesday each week, Cypress' CEO has a company-wide status report on employee performance based on their own targets. Just imagine what impact motivation has on such a process where employees know that at any moment the CEO might take a closer look at their area.

Can you see the Five Building Blocks at work?

1. **Communication** — Employees initiate and drive communication to center on their work efforts. Managers have ready access to understand quickly what is progressing and what is getting stalled.

2. **Developing Followers** — Followers are being developed to be leaders in their work. This system demands they assume responsibility for propelling their work forward. The focus is on delivering high-yield results for the company. The system can be sabotaged by overzealous micromanagers. To guarantee the integrity of employee-driven projects, management must resist becoming overengaged in the details and focus on key issues.

3. **Focus on Key Issues** — The weekly goal-setting and updating keep each individual focused on their contributions to the company. Managers review and troubleshoot all areas, seeking to identify conflicts, overlaps and slumps. Managers need to see what their workers need from them to excel.

4. **Link With Others** — This process is critical to provide an on-line update of where people are with their work for themselves and others. Anyone can review the status reports to understand how individuals, teams and the entire company is operating and under what expectations and goals.

5. **Personal and Professional Balance** — This process enables employees to have a wide-angle view of the company and to understand their contributions in terms of project success rather than job success. This seems a healthy view — to see how the project and the company are progressing rather than just to be mired in one's own work alone. Speed and flexibility occur more easily and allow individuals more of a vantage point to plan both their work and their personal agenda.

HANANFORD BROTHERS OF MAINE and WHOLE FOODS MARKETS IN TEXAS

These two companies utilize the team concept throughout the structuring, functioning and managing of their business. Like the Japanese, they believe the team is the central organizing concept of the business. Departmental teams buy and price what they sell. They have an immediacy to customers and keep track of preferences and emerging trends. In most food chains, these functions are seldom delegated to the store manager, let alone departments! The bottom-line impact on profitability is undeniably linked to engaging workers in the total productivity of each store. Departmental teams hire and fire co-workers, establish and monitor work rules and have significant input into the compensation system.

Can you see the Five Building Blocks at work?

1. **Communication** — Team members must communicate with customers and themselves in determining what products to carry and how to price and sell them. They collaborate with each other in developing work rules and in seeing to it they are enacted. Communication is central in recruiting and releasing co-workers and assures that the professional needs of the department and business are met, as well as the operating norms of the work culture.

C A S E   S T U D Y

45

2

2. **Developing Followers** — Followers lead the business at both companies. No universal, company-wide formula dictates ordering and merchandising in these companies. The followers are entrusted with the responsibility to identify customer needs and respond.

3. **Focus on Key Issues** — Departmental teams are front and center and have the charter to deliver results and service.

4. **Link With Others** — By making departmental teams the central organizing unit of the business, these two companies have made success co-dependent on collaboration. Cross-training is also a critical element of smooth functioning teams as is less reliance on a departmental head.

5. **Personal and Professional Balance** — Personal and professional balance may be served in this example because of team members' relatedness to one another and to customers. There is closer proximity to understanding lifestyle preferences and needs and therefore, perhaps, more insight and clarity related to one's own.

WAL-MART and VISA

These two organizations have created accelerated communication systems and championed information partnerships among their constituents. In an era where we have gone from information gathering to disseminating at near the speed of sound, Wal-Mart and VISA win the prize for utilizing technology to the fullest to keep everyone with a "need to know" informed about the business. Wal-Mart uses electronic data interchange to release sales data to the makers of the products it sells, who then are expected to replenish Wal-Mart's inventory automatically. VISA, the world's largest credit card brand, is owned by its 22,000 member banks and its other financial institutions. Built on innovation, it created the first system for banks to transfer money electronically to one another. VISA serves as a 21st-century model of how companies can extend their boundaries without the encumbrance of a cumbersome hierarchy. VISA is a focused federation that is only in business to please its customers and its constituents.

Can you see the Five Building Blocks at work?

1. **Communication** — On-line and instantaneous access have garnered market share and guaranteed immediacy of information. Efficiency and accuracy are necessary outputs of such systems.

2. **Developing Followers** — Followers have control of choices they make and have access to critical information that drives their business decisions.

3. **Focus on Key Issues** — The information link is a powerful one and creates autonomy and critical thinking on issues central to the business and its success.

4. **Link With Others** — The interrelationships established through such systems creates strategic partnerships that propel mutual success for years to come. Open information systems inspire trust, confidence and reciprocity.

5. **Personal and Professional Balance** — Is there a consumer who hasn't been supported by either Wal-Mart or VISA's reliability or dependability? Great electronic systems and access to them have certainly made going on vacation, completing home improvement projects, buying a new wardrobe and a host of other *personal* activities infinitely more easy. Members and vendors like doing business with Wal-Mart and VISA because these two organizations keep everyone on the same information screen — which seems like a pretty *balanced* way to do business.

2

C
A
S
E

S
T
U
D
Y

Three Kinds of Leaders

There is confusion within companies today related to who has responsibility for what. Structures and processes are being redefined and reconfigured rapidly only to be revamped again. Whole tiers of management have been thrown out. So many jobs have evaporated that the very concept of organizing work around a "job" may not survive to the year 2000. Never has the demand for leadership been so critical.

Companies are struggling with implementation concerns. People and their companies are accepting the reality of change and continue to do much to learn new processes and strategies to help them advance. However, one common theme among the companies is how to distribute leadership responsibility appropriately. We begin to address this question by looking at three kinds of leaders.

Do not think of these three kinds of leaders as three levels of leaders. Rather, think of their differentiation based on their contribution to propelling the business. Keep in mind that all three types of leaders utilize the **Five Building Blocks of Effective Leadership.** Note how we have assigned some areas of responsibility to the three types of leaders in the **diagram** of the **AIM Leadership Model.** The diagram is especially valuable for its overlays, where we demonstrate the three types of leaders across one axis and the key components and subheads of the model on the other. Then we begin to break down some specific areas of focus for each of the three types of leaders corresponding to the leadership initiatives of **action, influence and motivation.**

NOTE: We have not included a company's **Top Team** in the **AIM Leadership Model.** A company's Top Team — the chairman, CEO, president, CFO and other members of the company's senior corporate committee — have such distinct authority and power in the company that we do not address their full scope in this book. However, much of what we describe related to *Business Leaders* applies to the **Top Team.**

2

The **AIM Leadership Model** is based on three kinds of organizational leaders:

1. **Business Leaders** — Business leaders are responsible for "defining the playing field." They sign-off on the company's vision, mission and values. They develop a business and market strategy. They set broad challenges for the rest of the company's leadership. More than anything, these leaders are responsible for keeping a sharp focus on knowing and revisiting assumptions about "What business are we in?" Some leaders included in this broad category are: top leadership (CEOs, COOs, CFOs, etc.), division presidents and product leaders (R&D).

2. **Team Leaders** — Team leaders are responsible for "coaching the players." They focus the resources of the company and their work group or team to meet customer needs. They set specific goals and objectives which reflect the broader challenges from *business leaders* and continuously "move the bar" to improve standards and quality. They provide a key organizational role in linking the perspective and experience of *business leaders* and *individual leaders*. Some examples of team leaders are: department/staff function heads (accounting, human resources, purchasing, MIS, etc.), project managers and process leaders.

3. **Individual Leaders** — Individual leaders are responsible for "making the plays." They also call time-outs and provide great "heads-up" moves to alert other leaders of both operational and marketplace feedback. Their information may alter either the broader challenges from *business leaders* or specific goals and objectives which they form with *team leaders*. Specifically, they are responsible for assuring that the best processes and technology are being used in an optimal way to accomplish the work. Some individual leaders in this category include: cross-functional, cross-divisional and work-directed team members (process-improvement teams, new-product launch teams, integration teams), customer service group members and those directly engaged in making the product.

2

Creating Leadership Responsibility Throughout the Company

"Again and again the impossible problem is solved when we see that the problem is only a tough decision waiting to be made."
Robert Schuller

Companies know that the daily operating environment requires that people become increasingly prepared to handle a range of responses to very diverse circumstances. People operating in different capacities must be flexible in how they think and act in solving customer problems and using company resources.

The diagram reflects the essence of the **AIM Leadership Model** and illustrates how a company can apply leadership throughout its daily operating environment. The focus is on what specific actions the different types of leaders must take in the leadership mobilizing process. First, examine how the Top Team must set the stage and create a work environment in order for people to excel as leaders.

Taking AIM on Leadership Model

**Creating Leadership Responsibility
Throughout the Company**

Action
- Share a vision
- Create core values
- Manage change

Influence
- Clarify perceptions
- Build relationships
- Utilize influence appropriately

Leadership

Motivation
- Understand needs
- Give feedback/support
- Use motivation to encourage peak performance

2

The AIM Leadership Model

How Company Leaders Apply the AIM Model

	Business Leaders	Team Leaders	Individual Leaders
Action • Vision • Values • Change	Define the playing field	Coach the players	Execute the plays
Influence • Perceptions • Relationships • Styles	Create the playing field	Create individual and team roles	Be a role model
Motivation • Needs • Encouragement • Performance	Align rewards and recognition	Apply rewards and recognition	Excel at the work

Different types of leaders execute different *plays* on the playing field. The total work environment requires distinct leadership and specific initiative from all three types of leaders in the **AIM Leadership Model.** Consider how this model may get played out in your own work environment.

Who are your business leaders?_____
_____

Who are your team leaders?_____
_____

Who are your individual leaders?_____
_____

What Can the AIM Leadership Model Do for You?

We have developed the **AIM Leadership Model** to help you and your company answer four strategic questions regarding leadership requirements for today's companies:

1. What kind of leadership style and culture is required for your company to be successful?

2. What types of leaders are needed in your company?

3. What do these different kinds of leaders do, what are they responsible for and how do they share a continuum of responsibility?

4. How does your company move leadership throughout the organization?

   Keep these four questions in mind as you review the tips for creating leadership responsibility throughout the company.

Five Actions the Top Team Must Take

The Top Team of a company must successfully ready the work environment in order to set the stage for successful change and transition opportunities:

1. Lead a change process that will alter the way management and employees work together.

2. Re-examine leadership and identify what the company values and needs. Specify how it will develop and reward self-directed leadership throughout the organization.

3. Determine a strategic direction for the company as a whole.

4. Delegate the authority (along with the responsibility) to translate vision into action by people throughout the organization.

5. Define the standards for business success and expect other *business, team* and *individual leaders* to set their own performance goals and measures.

Five Actions Business Leaders Must Take

Business leaders in a company must accept specific responsibility to:

1. Create a vision of an ideal future company. Answer the question "What business are we in?"

2. Develop a mission and commit to a business and market strategy. Create, model and reward shared values.

3. Encourage the creation of flexible structures, provide the financing to acquire or develop resources and position the utilization of internal and external networks that operate informally.

2

4. Develop a range of leadership styles, be an aggressive learner, mentor others and establish a leadership-development continuum for the company. Listen, test assumptions and sharpen focus.

5. Align customer needs, company response and team and individual rewards.

Five Actions Team Leaders Must Take

Team leaders in a company must accept specific responsibility to:

1. Review the vision and mission, as well as gather and provide feedback related to customer, competitor and company experience.

2. Set measurable goals and objectives for the group as a whole and with individual team members. Model and reward shared values. Troubleshoot for breakdowns and discrepancies within their team and mediate resolutions.

3. Take advantage of business-leader initiative to create flexible structures, acquire and develop resources and use informal, internal and external networks. Facilitate and support the development of these three factors among team members.

4. Adapt and develop leadership styles to respond to group members and share leadership among team members. Listen, test assumptions and sharpen focus.

5. Develop models which demonstrate how customer needs, company response, and team and individual rewards are linked.

Five Actions Individual Leaders Must Take

Individual leaders must accept specific responsibility to:

1. Determine how they will work in tandem with others. They must scope out a personal contribution to their work group, team and business unit.

2. Set measurable goals and objectives in step with those of the work group, team or business unit. Operate by shared values.

3. Utilize and create flexible structures, acquire and develop resources, and use informal, internal and external networks. Share information and resources readily with others.

4. Identify what they need from other leaders. Adapt and develop their leadership style to work well with others. Learn to shift comfortably from leadership to followership. Listen, test assumptions and sharpen focus.

5. Discover how to link the fulfillment of individual needs and goals with those of customers, the team or work group, the business unit and the company. Recognize company response and rewards from other leaders.

Company Profile

How General Electric Is Creating Leadership Responsibility

Read through these brief descriptions of a few of the initiatives Jack Welch, Chairman and Chief Executive Officer of GE, is using in the transformation of General Electric. Share your responses to these questions and discuss them with other leaders at your company.

Profile of a Leader
General Electric: #1, #2 or Out

Jack Welch has led General Electric through a major transformation over the past 10 years. He has committed that the businesses that make up GE will be #1 or #2 in the industry — or they'll "get out of the business." During the last decade, Welch has made $21 billion in major acquisitions and divested GE of $11 billion of businesses which could not be #1 or #2.

GE's core values are speed, simplicity, self-confidence and integrity. Welch did not determine these alone or at lunch one day with other key executives. Instead, Welch asked Crotonville, the company's "think tank" and leadership-development mecca, to assess a wide range of management's perceptions of what values should guide GE into the next century. After nearly five years and input from thousands of managers and laundry lists of truly admirable values, Welch distills it all down to speed, simplicity, self-confidence and integrity.

Why spend five years asking the same question of so many people? Welch believes the participation is the real benefit. With so many people talking and debating about GE's core values for so long, the entire company influenced the emergence and practice of these values before Welch announced them. That's change from the inside out.

GE recruits people who will commit uncommon energy and dedication to being the best at what they do. Only the hearty need apply and while you're at it, be thinking about what your next contribution (not necessarily *promotion*) will be to GE *after* you successfully fill the role for which you are currently being recruited. GE is already thinking about it and won't recruit you if they see that you have no vision for what's next. Welch knows GE will grow in direct proportion to the boldness and innovation of its leaders.

Key Questions

Keep in mind the leadership of Jack Welch as you do this part of the exercise:

1. What kind of leader is he? Would he find the **AIM Leadership Model** useful? Why or why not? _____

   _____

2. What do GE's core values and the process Welch used to determine them say about his leadership? _____

   _____

3. What can you determine about his style? How might he adapt his style to different GE businesses? Contrast an industry leader and a business that is becoming obsolete in the U.S. _____

   _____

4. What do you think about GE's recruitment strategy? Will it attract the kind of leaders Welch wants? _____

   _____

5. What kind of leader does Welch want on his team? Could you sign on to his team? Why or why not? _____

   _____

Summary of AIM Leadership Model

2

According to MIT's Peter Senge, learning organizations are companies which "tone" their people to "flex around," *knowing* they are going in the right direction. Learning organizations nurture leadership behavior in all their members — top down, inside out. In today's quick-step, market-driven environment, one can see the need for leadership at all levels of an organization.

The **AIM Leadership Model** and diagram (on page 51) should help you understand **self-directed leadership** and the value of developing it throughout the organization. The diagram and accompanying descriptions demonstrate how leaders must sign on for specific responsibilities which are linked to all other leaders and the results of the entire company.

The model crystallizes top leadership's specific charter to authorize such a widely distributed delegation of responsibility and authority. Only top leaders can empower an organization to change and reinvent itself.

The **AIM Leadership Model** — **Action, Influence and Motivation** — demonstrates how a company can develop and sustain a motivational leadership process and clarifies:

- what function three different types of leaders fulfill for the company (business, team, and individual leaders)

- what responsibilities are unique and which overlap among a company's leadership

- how the company can mobilize people to lead

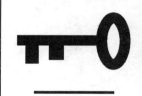

Commitment from the top is essential where those leaders serve as true models of the competencies and values they want practiced by all leaders. Business, team and individual leaders must accept the company's initiative and commit themselves to coach, mentor and reward one another and their colleagues for a shared process.

2

> *"It is more important to know where you are going than to get there quickly. Do not mistake activity for achievement."*
> Mabel Newcomer

If leadership is truly focused on "doing the right things," then all leaders have to observe and participate actively with the 3 Cs — Customers, Competition and Company. The **Five Building Blocks of Effective Leadership (Communication, Developing Followers, Focus on Important Issues, Link With Others** and **Personal and Professional Balance)** provide core behaviors for driving leadership development and practice along a continuum of service.

Companies now understand they must not seek "off the shelf" solutions for their leadership and workforce development programs. The collective experience of one's own organization and the experience of other companies will form a foundation from which to invent the future. But the real work of creating one's own destiny is a company-driven, creative process where all members must assume leadership. Yesterday's answers are not good enough for 21st-century solutions. Self-directed leadership throughout the organization requires good ears, willing hearts and keen minds ready to anticipate the future and learn what they don't know in order to meet the needs of customers through **Action, Influence** and **Motivation.**

Here is a sampling of what some companies and their people who are operating in work environments similar to those reflected in the **AIM Leadership Model** have to say about self-directed leadership:

"Do what is right. Get results. Do it together."
Twyla Morgan, Manager, Procter & Gamble

"I spend a lot of time working at participative management. But I have to be honest and say I think we get better decisions out of it."
Roger Smith, Former CEO of General Motors

"The most difficult thing at AT&T has been for some managers to give up control. The managers that are making it are learning to unleash creativity in their people."
Joseph Jalarreau, Director of Executive Education, AT&T

"If you really believe in quality, when you cut through everything, it's empowering your people that leads to teams. Regardless of the business you are in, teams are critical to achieving the work of the future."
Jamie Houghton, CEO, Corning, Inc.

"The worst thing you can do to a team is to leave it alone in the dark. I guarantee if you come across someone who says teams didn't work in their company, it's because management didn't take an interest in them."
James Watson, Vice President, Texas Instruments

"(Jack) Welch's success as a leader depends less on his personality than on the quality of his thoughts. Smart, intellectually disciplined and creative. The 20th century has produced two business leaders who will be remembered for their ideas: Alfred Sloan of General Motors and Jack Welch of GE."
Noel Tichy, Former GE Management Educator at Crotonville

"The greatest power we have is the ability to envision our own fate and to change ourselves."
Jack Welch, CEO, General Electric

Questions for Personal Development

1. What is the major emphasis of this chapter?

_____

_____

_____

_____

2. What are the most important things you learned from this chapter?

_____

_____

_____

_____

3. How can you apply what you learned to your current job?

_____

_____

_____

_____

4. How will you go about making these changes?

_____

_____

_____

_____

5. How can you monitor improvement?

_____

_____

_____

_____

6. Summarize the changes you expect to see in yourself one year from now.

_____

_____

_____

_____

CHAPTER 3

Leadership and Action

One of the most admired descriptions of leaders is that they are action-oriented — and that they produce results. The leaders of today are being asked to achieve more difficult goals — in shorter periods of time. What the most successful leaders have learned is that they must be focused on where they want to go. Secondly, they must recognize the value of their people and seek their participation in shaping the future.

Specifically, leaders focus on the following key areas to produce results:

- **Provide direction** by sharing a vision of what can be achieved at a point in the future. Leaders are able to link business strategy to the team and individual goals of the employees who work with them.
- **Establish core values** which help to shape positive behavior. This often helps to inspire people, by integrating personal and company values.
- **Manage change and transitions** through people. They are able to remove barriers and resistance which can inhibit top performance.

The best leaders know that success is achieved by linking individual contributions with business plans and strategies. Action-oriented leaders can create the environment for this to occur.

3

Creating Direction Through Vision

Leaders often ask, "What is vision? Isn't it just another name for a mission statement? Isn't it the same exercise we've done over and over again. You know, creating a lot of ideas, putting a lot of paper on the walls and then forgetting about it until next year? Then, why is vision so important to the success of our business?"

Vision is critical to successfully move your organization in the right direction. Vision is a clear, concise and simple statement of what the organization is trying to accomplish and what you want it to become. It is the tool which guides people as they shape plans for their teams, departments or individual objectives. By expressing a vision, leaders create a focus on the future in which people want to participate.

Making the Vision Come Alive

How can a powerful vision statement be created? The concept is fairly simple. People must be involved in helping to shape the vision and to develop a plan on how the vision can be implemented. You will find that through discussions of vision involving your people, they will commit to doing things they have never done before.

Leaders create vision by preparing a compelling and inspiring statement of the direction for the organization.

Some examples of vision statements include:

Motorola. Chairman Robert W. Galvin's first vision was for a ten-fold improvement in quality. Today, Motorola has adopted a vision of achieving "Six Sigma." Six Sigma is a statistical term that translates to 3.4 defects for one million parts produced or, in other words, products that are 99.9998 percent free of defects. No U.S. company has ever reached that goal. However, the company was able to translate Galvin's vision into a measurable, realistic output and is currently operating at about 5.2 Sigma. When the program was first started, the company was at 4.0 Sigma. Its vision continues to be Six Sigma.

C
A
S
E

S
T
U
D
Y

Walt Disney. Everyone who attends will be treated as a guest. You are not a tourist; you are not another number — you are a guest with a capital "G." They spend time, money and energy in making sure their people recognize this vision. The managers talk about it. New employees are hired and spend weeks in training, learning about this guest-relations approach. If you have ever been to any of the Disney amusement parks, you know the excellent results they have achieved.

NASA (1960). "To launch the New Frontier." This vision was partially achieved in 1969, when NASA achieved the moon landing.

The Visions of Great Leaders

Throughout history the great leaders have been able to shape the way people think, feel and act by sharing their visions of the future. Some of the best examples are from politics, business and various professions.

Winston Churchill. This British statesman held several cabinet posts during 1906–1929. He became Great Britain's prime minister in 1939. His vision guided Great Britain and the allies through World War II to victory.

Churchill's Vision
"Victory of democracy over tyranny."

3

Martin Luther King, Jr. Martin Luther King accepted a major role in the difficult struggle for black civil rights in America. His followers were large in number and represented many races, as well. His mission was to end segregation, but his vision of the future provided a rallying cry for millions of Americans.

> **Martin Luther King, Jr.'s Vision**
> "Equality for all. From every
> mountaintop, let freedom ring."

Florence Nightingale. Florence Nightingale served as a role model for the nursing profession in the late 1850s. She believed that a strong medical system was critical to the delivery of health care to its patients. She also believed in the highest standards for all medical personnel.

> **Florence Nightingale's Vision**
> A healthcare system which is run with high
> professional standards for doctors and nurses.

Thomas J. Watson, Sr. Tom Watson joined a computer company which later became IBM. Under his leadership the company grew into international markets by focusing on excellence in product development, sales and support activities. He believed that the company should function as one large family and motivated employees to want to be part of it.

> **Tom Watson's Vision**
> A world-class organization which would last
> forever, producing business machines that
> operated at the speed of light.

Team leaders and individual leaders can help shape their company vision by explaining what the vision means to them and the people they work with. The goal is to have every employee in the organization understand the vision and be able to explain how their job is helping to accomplish it.

How to Create Your Own Vision

Creating the vision is one of the most inspirational projects a leader can undertake. If backed up with action (e.g., business and customer strategy, company employee policies), it is a powerful motivator in the work environment. If not, a vision statement is worthless. The ability to capture a picture of the organization which people can follow in a compelling vision statement is key to aligning employees behind a unified direction for the future. A vision statement is a guide for direction setting and business planning throughout the company.

The Company Vision. The company vision statement is normally developed by the top leadership team which would include the CEO or president. This vision statement represents the potential to link the top of the organization with all employees. This vision statement is a springboard for all other company leaders to shape their individual visions.

If your company has a vision statement, you should take advantage of using it to shape your own vision. If your company does not have a vision statement, you might consider using a quality policy or mission statement as a starting point.

Refer to the following sample quality policy:

WE are dedicated to exceeding the expectations of our internal and external customers with uncompromising integrity.

In a participative environment of continuous improvement, our commitment is to satisfy our customers by providing error-free products and services every time.

QUALITY is the most important element of our business.

If you are developing a vision statement with only limited information, consider utilizing this background. Here are a few thought-provoking questions:

What do your customers and others consider to be your strategic advantage?

_____
_____
_____

What major improvement or value-added service or direction do you want to provide?

_____
_____
_____
_____

What basic belief or calling do you want your employees to follow?

_____
_____
_____
_____

What will help distinguish you in your customers' eyes?

_____
_____
_____
_____

Identify any individual leaders (champions) who are shaping the vision and direction of your company, unit or team. How do they reflect the company or group's vision?

_____
_____
_____
_____

Creating Your Vision Statement

After reviewing your company vision or utilizing the input from the questions you just answered, complete the "Creating Your Vision Statement." Then, summarize your thoughts into one cohesive statement. Review the examples of vision statements of other companies presented earlier in this chapter.

3

We are ... *(make this first sentence inspiring, strategic, compelling)*

creating ...

_____

_____

designing ...

_____

_____

building ...

_____

_____

In such a way ... *(the method you are considering)*

_____

_____

_____

_____

So that ... *(the results you want; the changes that need to occur)*

_____

_____

_____

_____

As measured by ... *(How will you know when you get there? What will the organization culture be like? What will the product be like? What will people say and do?)*

_____

_____

_____

_____

"Creating Your Own Vision Statement" is used with permission from Sheila Connor, Performance Dynamics.

Summarize Your Vision Statement

Write a brief paragraph that captures the essence of your vision.

Testing and Shaping Your Vision

Once you have drafted a vision statement, it is important to share it with your colleagues, team members or co-workers. This will give you a feeling of how credible your vision is and a reading as to its potential to guide future direction.

Be patient in seeking participation and input. Be sure to convey your desire for ideas and be flexible to use them if they can help to clarify your vision. This is a very powerful step and will make your final vision statement much more inspiring.

If your company does not have a vision statement, you should share it with your business leaders for possible use in developing a broader company vision.

Implementing Vision

Once you have confirmed a vision, while getting input and support from other colleagues and employees, the challenge shifts to how to implement the vision.

The power of vision becomes more obvious when you consider the impact of linking business planning and customer-driven service. A company which aligns all of its internal resources (human and technical) behind a clear vision and sense of purpose already has captured the energy and motivation of its workforce. This is central to increasing market share and maintaining dependable quality and service.

When the competition — both domestic and global — is so significant, it is no time to become unfocused. Implementing the vision is the best shot companies have to be seen and valued in the very busy marketplace. Think of the magnitude of the results that are possible when the collective efforts of the entire organization are focused in the same direction!

> *"The leader must know, must know that he knows and must be able to make it abundantly clear to those about him that he knows."*
> Clarence B. Randall

3

From Vision to Action

To move from vision to action, an organization must develop:

1. **A framework for action**
2. **Commitment from employees**
   - Participation
   - Mutual goal-setting
   - High performance expectations
3. **Communication strategy**

Framework for Action

The framework for action incorporates a vision for the future and the strategies and plans to make it happen. Involving people at all levels of the organization is crucial to the success of this process. The external input of customers and suppliers is also a requirement to ensure that the end results will match the company's vision and performance expectations.

The *Framework for Action* Flow Chart (page 74) is one which can be shared throughout the organization. The chart will help people understand how to deploy the vision and then develop business strategies and link team and individual goals that are aligned with the company's vision.

Commitment From Employees

Engaging business group and team members early in the vision and strategy process is essential to energizing people to *commit to change and transition*. People are always more productive when they *participate* fully in work decisions, problem-solving and creating processes related to achieving results. Participation marks the difference between a workforce that is *told* what to do and one which *thinks* about what needs to be done.

3

One of the most powerful strategies a company can implement in moving vision to action is to create a mechanism throughout the organization for mutual goal-setting. Aligning people behind the vision and a core set of values gets real muscle when individuals and work teams set business goals that optimize a company's strengths and accelerate its mission. Such an energized operational environment creates a message that high performance expectations are the norm. Peers support this phenomenon readily in companies that are deliberately moving from vision to action.

Communication Strategy

The company must also develop a supporting communication strategy in order to effectively move itself from vision to action. The lack of adequate and timely communication is typically the number one complaint among a company's workforce. When companies are going through change and transition, they need to focus more than ever on what needs to be communicated to whom and when and how.

Taking time to develop a well-thought-through communication strategy will make all the difference between a vision that is isolated at the top and one that is claimed by employees everywhere in the company. Use appropriate communication vehicles, such as meetings (both general, division and team), questionnaires, issue-related feedback sheets, self-reports, assessments, customer meetings, focus groups, satisfaction reports and newsletters. The time you spend in keeping the organization informed is nothing compared to the time you might have to spend repairing damage from not communicating.

> *"Ignorance is not bliss—it is oblivion."*
> Philip Wylie

Framework for Action Flow Chart

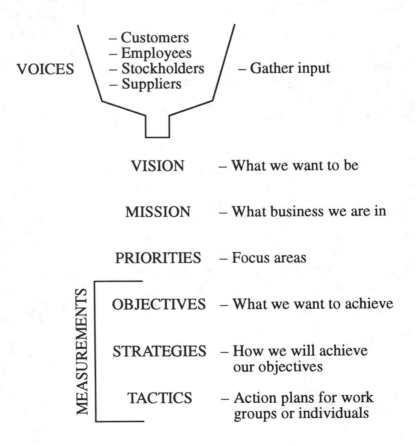

VOICES	– Customers – Employees – Stockholders – Suppliers	– Gather input
	VISION	– What we want to be
	MISSION	– What business we are in
	PRIORITIES	– Focus areas
MEASUREMENTS	OBJECTIVES	– What we want to achieve
	STRATEGIES	– How we will achieve our objectives
	TACTICS	– Action plans for work groups or individuals

It is important to share this framework with the entire organization to ensure that everyone has the same understanding of how to deploy the vision.

Communicating the Framework for Action

When communicating the framework for action, it is important to explain the purpose of each category. This framework can be utilized by business leaders to complete vision, mission and priorities. Team leaders can enhance the planning process by completing objectives and strategies to help implement the vision.

Voices and Vision: The link to creating a vision which will lead to exciting results in the marketplace is through the voice of customers, employees, stockholders and suppliers. These inputs will help shape and create a successful vision.

Mission: The purpose of the organization. Helps to determine the core businesses and services you are in.

Priorities: Many projects and ideas are feasible; therefore, the organization must discipline itself on the "focused few" so it will not dilute the implementation and execution of the vision.

Objectives and Strategies: Should deal with specific, measurable objectives for projects necessary to achieve the vision and the strategy to get there. Objectives are the "whats" and strategies are the specific "hows."

Tactics: Specific actions or activities for each strategy. They should tie directly into the achievement of the strategy. Tactics are usually sequential and are related to a timeline or schedule.

Key Measurements: Contain the cost, quality, quantity, timing and service requirements. The specific measurements to be used will depend on the project. These measures should be applied to both individuals and teams.

> *"Coming together is a beginning; keeping together is progress; working together is success."*
> Henry Ford

Vision to Action Planner

Example

Vision: To be the recognized leader in all market segments, we compete for low-cost, high-quality and superior service.

Mission: To design and manufacture products which meet customer needs and create customer satisfaction and loyalty.

Priorities:
- Increase market share
- Increase profitability
- Increase customer satisfaction

Objectives/Strategies:
- Introduce 10 new products ahead of the competition in 1997
- Reduce cycle times by 40 percent
- Reduce accounts-receivable days outstanding by 30 percent
- Negotiate new terms
- Achieve 100 percent service level (on-time deliveries)

Tactics: Improve automatic distribution network

Measurements:
Sales revenue 1996 vs. 1997
Number of new products introduced
Operating income before taxes
Customer-satisfaction measures

Keys to Implementing the Vision

pər-tis-ə-pa-shən
1. The act of participating.
2. The state of being related to a larger whole.

Critical to the process is participation. Research in this area confirms — and it makes a great deal of common sense — **people like to be a part of defining their job and the objective-setting process and will work harder toward objectives that they have a hand in developing.** Participation should begin in the planning stage and continue throughout the performance and evaluation of one's job.

"Never tell people how to do things. Tell them what to do and they will surprise you with their ingenuity." Gen. George Patton

Mutual Goal-Setting

After the Top Team shares the vision and priorities, business leaders, team leaders and individuals then have the opportunity to define their objectives, strategies, tactics and measurements. If the team or individuals are unskilled in preparing these plans, the leader should utilize the appropriate style in supporting them.

Leadership Styles in Action

How Leadership Styles Affect Goal Setting

Action	Autocratic	Democratic/ Participative	Free-Rein	Blended
Goal Setting	Leader tells followers what the expected results are to be	Mutual goal-setting	Followers present their goals	Leader sets direction. Gives responsibility based on skills

Setting High Expectations

There has been much written about how your expectations of others actually shape their behavior. Consider this example from Dr. Sterling Livingston's article "Pygmalion in Management."

An experiment involving 60 preschool students in a summer Headstart program compared the performance of pupils under:

1. Teachers who had been led to expect relatively slow learning by their children and
2. Teachers who had been led to believe their children had excellent intellectual abilities.

In fact, there was no difference in the abilities of the two groups. However, the pupils under the second group of teachers learned much faster.

This experiment is played out in a number of different settings, including business and sports. There are numerous examples in the sales profession where the leader/boss expectations actually determined the sales ability of the sales representatives. In sports, a disappointed coach who feels he has average players will often see his team never get above a 50 percent winning average.

What has been learned about this phenomenon?

- What the leader expects of subordinates and the way they are treated most likely will determine their performance.
- A characteristic of outstanding leaders is their ability to establish high expectations that their subordinates are able to meet.
- Leaders who fail to develop these same expectations see a productivity drop in their subordinates.
- Subordinates, more often than not, appear to perform in a manner in which they feel they are expected to by their leader.

In reviewing the notes about high expectations, business leaders, team leaders and individual leaders should raise their level of expectation to support people toward higher performance levels.

Creating Core Values

Values and beliefs are critical dimensions in leadership effectiveness, serving as a key for direction and action. The formation of an organization is marked by the making of value commitments in which leaders are primarily experts in the promotion and protection of values. Thomas Watson, Jr., the genius behind IBM, had a similar view, for he believed that an organization must have a strong set of beliefs on which it bases all policies and actions.

> *"If you treat an individual as he is, he will stay as he is, but if you treat him as if he were what he ought to be and could be, then he will become what he ought to be and what he could be."*
> Johann Wolfgang von Goethe

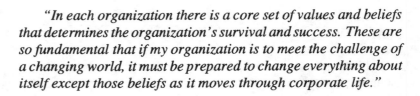

"In each organization there is a core set of values and beliefs that determines the organization's survival and success. These are so fundamental that if my organization is to meet the challenge of a changing world, it must be prepared to change everything about itself except those beliefs as it moves through corporate life."

In their book, *In Search of Excellence*, Peters and Waterman describe the seven basic beliefs shared by the excellent companies they studied:

1. Belief in being the best
2. Belief in the importance of the details of execution, the nuts and bolts of doing the job well
3. Belief in the importance of people as individuals
4. Belief in superior quality and service
5. Belief that most members of the organization should be innovators, and its corollary, the willingness to support failure
6. Belief in the importance of informality to enhance communication
7. Belief in and recognition of the importance of economic growth and profits

One of the most important challenges of leaders is to help clarify values and ensure that their values are consistent with those of the company.

Values

Values ... those beliefs reflected in demonstrated behavior which reflect what you consider important for how you should function.

Values comprise the beliefs that are most important to us. They are the deep-seated, pervasive standards that influence almost every aspect of our lives — our moral judgments, our responses to others, our commitments to personal and organizational goals.

It is our values that give direction to the hundreds of decisions made at all levels of the organization every day. Options that run counter to the company's values system are seldom considered.

Values constitute our personal "bottom line" ... and provide a prism through which all behavior is ultimately viewed.

Used by permission from *The Leadership Challenge: How to Get Extraordinary Things Done in Organizations*, p. 190–191, by James M. Kouzes and Barry Z. Posner. Copyright 1987, Jossey–Bass, Inc., publishers.

Sorting Out Your Values

One way to get in touch with what you want from your work is to identify some of your values and determine how strongly you feel about them.   Values are those social, moral and ethical standards that have been acquired over a lifetime and which underlie every decision and every course of action.

Problems arise when we must make choices that involve conflicting values. In the working world, for instance, one may have to choose between accepting a promotion that would require extensive overtime and travel versus staying where one is, sacrificing the promotion in order to spend more time with family and civic activities.

Often the amount of satisfaction we derive from our work is determined by the extent to which we can act out our values in our job.

"Character is that which reveals moral purpose, exposing the class of things a man chooses or avoids."
Aristotle

Values List

Affiliation	Loyalty
Security	Creative Expression
Friendship	Fast Pace
Independence	Helping Others
Work with Others	Challenging Problems
Status	Change and Variety
Achievement	Exercise Competence
Aesthetics	Recognition
Work Alone	Participation
Stability	Customer Contact
Excitement	Adventure
Balance	High Earnings
Job Tranquility	Health
Pressure	Competition
Frontiers of Knowledge	Physical Challenge
Fame	Precision Work
Time Freedom	Flexibility
Power and Authority	Family Happiness
Quality	Order
Personal Development	Integrity

This list contains commonly held values. Your task is to select 10 of the items that you ALWAYS or ALMOST ALWAYS value and five or more items that you SELDOM or NEVER value. List these items in the spaces provided. Think about why you made the choice you made. Next, reduce the list of the 10 most valued items to five and rank them. To what extent are you able to act out these values in your current job?

3

Always or Almost Always Valued Items

_____   _____

_____   _____

_____   _____

_____   _____

_____   _____

Seldom or Never Valued Items

_____   _____

_____   _____

_____   _____

_____   _____

_____   _____

Values Rank Order

1st _____   4th_____

2nd _____   5th _____

3rd _____

Now complete the same exercise, this time using what you perceive your company's values to be. Place the company values in the top five rank order.

Company Values

Always or Almost Always Valued Items

_____   _____

_____   _____

_____   _____

_____   _____

_____   _____

Seldom or Never Valued Items

_____   _____

_____   _____

_____   _____

_____   _____

_____   _____

Company Values Rank Order

1st _____

2nd _____

3rd _____

4th_____

5th _____

Answer the following questions to determine how closely aligned your own values and your company's are:

1. Is there a gap between my personal values and those of the organization? _____

   _____

   _____

2. How can I reconcile the values gap? _____

   _____

   _____

3. How can I use the values to guide my behavior? _____

   _____

   _____

   _____

4. How can I use these values as a leader to shape team and individual behavior? _____

   _____

   _____

How Core Values Guide Action

The purpose of values is to use them to guide action and behavior. When the values are aligned with the company vision, the result is a powerful force toward exceeding business plans.

One key business leader at Becton Dickinson and Company developed these core values to kick-off a leadership-development program:

Quality
- The customers we serve in virtually every market are very quality-conscious. Quality is defined by the products we sell and the services we provide.
- Every customer interaction is an opportunity to prove our quality.
- High quality is not an option ... it is a necessity.

Flexibility

- We serve many different customers with many different products in many different markets.
- This level of service and multitude of efforts requires flexibility.
- Flexibility is not an option ... it is a necessity.

Problem-Solving

- We are fundamentally in the business of solving problems for our customers and for our fellow workers.
- Problems are everywhere, every day. Every problem we encounter is an opportunity to serve.
- Being a problem-solver is not an option ... it is a necessity.

Your role as a leader is to enable your employees to act out the following values.

- Problem-solving
- High-quality performance
- Ability to change
- Ability to be flexible and adaptive

Our success as an organization and your success as individuals will be measured by how well you enable employees to act out these company values.

Understanding your personal and company values is an important first step. The key to becoming a leader at any level of an organization is to use these values to guide your day-to-day behavior and actions.

"Efforts and courage are not enough without purpose and direction."
John F. Kennedy

Company Profile

GE's Statement of Values

Here are some samples from GE's Statement of Values formulated over several years and written from the contributions of thousands of managers coming to Crotonville:

- Only satisfied customers can provide job security.

- Change is continual, thus nothing is sacred. Change is accepted as the rule rather than the exception.

- Paradox is a way of life. You must function collectively as one company and individually as many businesses at the same time. For us, leadership means leading while being led, producing more output with less input.

- We encourage the sharing of these values because we believe they are both fair and effective but we realize they are not for everyone ... Individuals whose values do not coincide with these expressed preferences will more likely flourish better outside the General Electric Company.

Key Questions

1. What do you think about the last point in the *Statement of Values?*

2. Write your own *Statement of Values* as it relates to your company. Share it with your co-workers and get their feedback. Then, write one that reflects your combined thinking.

_____

_____

_____

*C
A
S
E

S
T
U
D
Y*

3

87

3

Managing Change and Transitions

Not only is everything changing, but the rate of change is accelerating. The management of change has become another critical responsibility of leaders in today's dynamic organizations.

Corporate priorities can change overnight, especially with new leadership. The role of company leaders is to manage people through these changes and transitions while maintaining productivity and avoiding chaos. This challenge of experiencing the instability of change and still performing at optimum levels is facing all leaders in dynamic organizations. The notion of steady or predictable sales, customers, forecasts, etc., is being replaced by responding to the unexpected. It will be your role as a leader to provide a stabilizing influence as changes occur.

Flexibility is key in leading and participating in change cycles and providing support and direction for colleagues and employees. Leaders are continually moving toward the vision of the company business group or team as they respond to customer needs in a changing marketplace.

> *"To do nothing is the way to be nothing."*
> Nathaniel Howe

Personal Experience with Change

Briefly define change in connection with your work.

_____

_____

_____

_____

During the past two years, identify the changes you have experienced:

_____Reorganization of my department
_____New reporting relationships
_____Modifications in the product line
_____New technology
_____Reduction in force
_____Introduction of a new process
_____Addition of new equipment
_____Major policy revisions
_____Introduction of a new product
_____Centralization
_____Decentralization
_____Computerization
_____New work standards
_____Transfer to a new work group
_____Changes in the hours of work
_____Relocation of the office or plant
_____Revision of the pay system
_____Introduction of a new performance-appraisal system

Add Your Own

_____

_____

_____

How Leaders Approach Change

Think about the changes that have occurred in your life over the past two years. Which change was most difficult? Did you resist the change at any point? What factors helped you to make the change? Consider these key points as you reflect on these questions.

Planning for Change

As leaders prepare to make a change, either personally or with a team, there will always be some uncertainty about the chance for success.

As a leader, you should view the change process by asking three questions:

1. **What is the future vision?**
2. **Where am I today?**
3. **What must be done to manage the transition?**

You might use this simple model to plan ahead:

Change Model

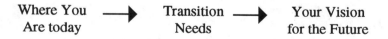

| Where You Are today | → | Transition Needs | → | Your Vision for the Future |

Planning process: Consider managing the change by analyzing the change model.

1. What is your vision for the future? Describe the optimum situation, if everything goes according to your expectations. Describe specifically what the new situation would look like.

    Example: A company was recently upgrading and automating its service-center operations. The regional director's vision for this change was a fully automated service center where customer waiting time is five minutes or less.

3

2. Where are you today? Describe the current situation, considering current productivity levels, available equipment, employee skill levels and commitment to your vision.

   Example: A manufacturing plant was planning to centralize its material-planning function to gain cost efficiency. The morale was low because employees felt that their jobs would be affected. This hurt productivity levels. Many employees did not commit to the vision because they did not understand the long-term implications of the change.

3 What must be done to successfully manage the transition? Describe your needs and concerns about the transition. List what you believe will be the most difficult parts of the change to deal with. Identify the key groups and individuals who have a vested interest, or stake, in the change. Finally, describe the issues, needs, and concerns of those who will be impacted most by the change. You may want to ask some of the individuals directly about their concerns — don't just assume from your observations.

Managing the Transition

Some of the earmarks of the transition period are:

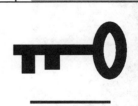

- High stress level
- Conflict increases
- Decrease in productivity

Much of the negative effect of change is due to individual resistance to the change. This may be caused by a lack of understanding of the change or their comfort level with the status quo. Your job as a leader will be to overcome resistance and ensure a smooth transition to your vision or desired goal.

Techniques to Lead People Through a Transition

Consider these techniques to ensure that everyone affected by the change is getting the support they need to respond in a positive way. It is largely through these individual efforts that the changes will be made and the vision achieved.

1. Try to let people know as far in advance as possible about the changes.
2. Describe the changes as completely as possible.
3. Avoid making changes that are not critical.
4. Provide appropriate training in new skills and concepts.
5. Make each person accountable for some aspect of the change.
6. Give special help to those who find it the most difficult to make the change.
7. Encourage people to think and act creatively.
8. Look for the positive "opportunities" created by the change.
9. Celebrate success as the changes fall into place.

Summary

No matter what your current level of leadership in your organization — individual, team or business leader — you will need to be responsible for positive actions. This is most critical when you have direct responsibility to lead others.

All successful leaders are able to express a vision and use that vision to drive performance through action. Core values support both the vision and the behavior of the company. When values are understood and consistently applied, they are a powerful guide for all employees.

Finally, leaders must manage change and transitions through people. A planned approach will create positive results and reduce chaos and confusion in moving toward a vision of the future.

3

"The thing to do is supply light and not heat."
Woodrow Wilson

93

Questions for Personal Development

1. What is the major emphasis of this chapter?

_____

_____

_____

_____

2. What are the most important things you learned from this chapter?

_____

_____

_____

_____

3. How can you apply what you learned to your current job?

_____

_____

_____

_____

4. How will you go about making these changes?

_____

_____

_____

_____

5. How can you monitor improvement?

_____

_____

_____

_____

6. Summarize the changes you expect to see in yourself one year from now.

_____

_____

_____

_____

CHAPTER 4

Leadership and Influence

4

When you think of influence, what comes to mind? Often you'll think of a political leader who exerts influence on his party members to gain acceptance for his or her point of view. You might also think of a business person trying to get employees to make an unpopular change in their work schedule. Both are examples of individuals using influence to convince others to take a desired course of action.

Influence Without Authority

Leaders in today's business environment are often called on to use influence to convince co-workers or colleagues to take action on a specific project knowing that they do not have the formal authority to direct the activities of these individuals. The responsibility to use this type of influence falls on team leaders and individual leaders more frequently. Businesses may even be required to influence people in other parts of the company who do not work directly for them. In moving from a vision to an implementation plan, leaders must realize that people will not automatically take the desired action which has been outlined.

To develop your influence skills, it is necessary to think about influence as a process. Think about a salesperson who is preparing to close a sale. The major goal is to convince the customer to buy a product or service. The salesperson is trying to convince the buyer to take action. The very best sales people follow a specific process to "close the deal." The process of using influence in business has some of these same requirements.

Let's take a look at the elements of using influence as a process and then break them down, individually, to learn how to apply them in day-to-day situations.

How Leaders Approach Influence

Let's assume that you have been assigned the leadership responsibility for making an improvement in your company. A small team has been formed to assist you to accomplish this task. You would most likely become the leader of a corrective-action team.

In following the AIM model, you would have established specific direction for the team under the action planning required of all effective leaders. You have learned that by "just" communicating the plan, some team members are not beginning to take the desired action you see as necessary for the results to be achieved.

What approach would you take?

Four Steps to Increasing Influence

When a leader notices that an individual or team needs more specific direction, the following steps can help to convince the individual or team to take the desired action.

"Trust men and they will be true to you; treat them greatly, and they will show themselves great."
Ralph Waldo Emerson

96

1. **Understand the situation.** Make sure that you have the whole story. One method of ensuring that you have an accurate view of the situation requires you to test your perceptions. Utilize active listening to gather information.

2. **Identify specific issues.** List the obstacles or barriers which are preventing individuals from taking action.

3. **Develop a strategy.** Based on your clear understanding of the issues, make an action plan of how you will influence the individual(s). Include:

    •A specific objective to be achieved
    •Positive outcomes expected
    •Potential resistance expected
    •Execution plan? Where and when

4. **Implement your plan,** using appropriate style(s) of influence.

Activating the Influence Model

Understanding the situation.

Utilizing perceptions can be an excellent method of assessing your work environment. This will help you gain an understanding of the barriers which can stand in the way of explaining why individuals are not producing results.

Check your perceptions on the next page ...

PERCEPTIONS

Understanding the situation.
What do you see?

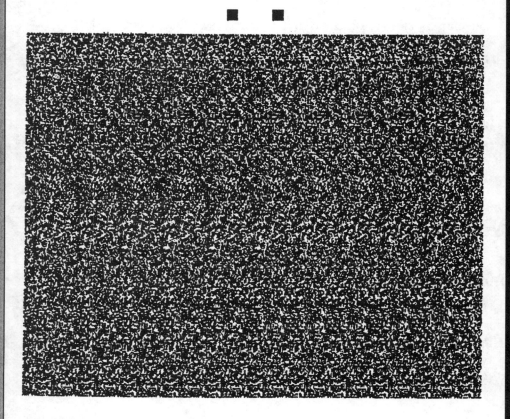

Find the 3-D picture. (Hold the picture about 6" away from your
eyes and focus for several minutes.)

Summary

The picture hidden in the graphic is a light bulb! Did you see it?

If not, how would you get help to see the picture if it was essential information for you?

The important factor is the amount of information we can build into our perceptions about a particular person or situation.

Use perceptions to gain an objective view of the situation by applying the following:

1. **Self-assessment:** Think about your own perceptions. What are your assumptions based upon? Are you viewing the situation through a filter? Talk with others to help test your perceptions.

2. **Walk in the other person's "shoes."** Make an effort to actively listen to the others. Put yourself in their place. Try to sense their position. Use active listening to "get the whole story."

3. **Reconcile differences.** Make every effort to modify your position, if the situation allows for it.

Increase Your Active Listening Skills

What Is Active Listening?

Active listening is the ability to hear a message clearly, using your eyes, ears and complete concentration. Consider these techniques for self-improvement.

- Prepare to listen — send listening signals
  - **welcoming signals** — show that you want to talk to the person
  - **attention signals** — both vocal and non-verbal, show that you are listening ("hmm," nod your head, etc.)

- Control distractions — barriers to listening
  - looking away, shifting objects, yawning, sitting at a distance, answering the phone, tapping a pencil, etc.

- Listen to the entire message — take time to listen and probe for information
  "Tell me more"
  "What else should I know?"
  "What makes this so important?"
  "How did this situation come about?"
  "For example?"

- Reinforce the communicator with non-verbal cues like nodding and smiling, and verbal ones such as
  "I understand"
  "That's a powerful insight"
  "You've given this a lot of thought"
  "I would like to know more"

- Confirm the message — playback
  "If I understand you correctly ..."
  "I hear you saying that ..."
  "So, what happened is ..."
  "The situation, then, is ..."

- Continue to monitor your listening skills.

Better Understanding Through Active Listening

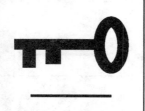

1. **What is said and done — day to day — is the most important part of communicating.** Intellectual honesty, living what is said and acting cooperatively are essential to developing good communications.

2. One of the **biggest obstacles** to communication **is the tendency to evaluate, to pass judgment on and to agree or disagree with statements before you find out what is meant.**

3. When listening, **look for what the speaker intends,** not just at what is said. Examine whether anything is being said "between the lines."

4. Ask more questions to see whether your listeners have understood what is intended. Have your instructions repeated, **"to see if I've said what I meant."** Check for understanding at the time of talking.

5. Misunderstandings are inevitable, and, therefore, the kind of atmosphere needs to be created that will **encourage people to ask questions** when they don't fully understand.

6. Where difficulties have arisen, try to keep the talking centered on **the problem rather than on personalities.**

7. Remember, **how the other person sees the situation is very often right.**

8. Where individuals disagree, **get each to state the other's position,** each to the satisfaction of the other. You should do this in your individual communication as well.

9. Recognize that, in discussions, disagreements are normal and inevitable. Expect it, prepare for it and use it to obtain greater awareness of the various aspects of the problem at hand.

10. Take every honest opportunity **to make the other person feel better or more important.**

11. When talking, **pause more often to think through what you are about to say.** You create strong impressions by the way you phrase ideas, such as whether you make rambling or concise statements.

12. **Tone of voice** is more important than you think. Consider what impressions you are conveying with your voice.

Bases of Power Used to Influence Others

Power is the ability to influence others and change their behavior to achieve specific action. Bases of power may occur at every level of the organization and are not limited by a certain position in the organization. There are five bases of power available to leaders:

1. **Legitimate Power** is created by the authority or position given to a person in the organization. Legitimate power is usually recognized as a "right" to influence. This fits best within a supervisor-subordinate relationship.

2. **Reward Power** is based on the ability of a person to influence others through the use of rewards. The rewards work best to reinforce actions, not as "bribes" to force action.

3. **Expert Power** is based on the perception that the person has important knowledge or experience not possessed by another individual or team.

4. **Referent Power** is created by the desire of an individual or team to identify with the influencer. These are usually individuals who develop as role models because of their special traits and abilities.

5. **Coercive Power** is the opposite of reward power and is based on the ability of the person to use punishment to influence specific actions. Coercive power has little or no use in today's empowered and customer-focused organizations.

4

Typical Bases of Power for Company Leaders

Business Leaders	Team Leaders	Individual Leaders
• Legitimate power	• Expert power	• Expert power
• Reward power	• Referent power	• Referent power
• Coercive power	• Reward power	

Maximize Your Use of Power to Influence Others

The use of power and influence has both positive and negative outcomes. The negative use of power and influence will create a win-lose environment. The use of power and influence is seen as manipulative and also creates limited results in terms of maximizing productivity. Individuals and teams often repel the use of negative power and influence and will only do "what is required" instead of "what is possible" when working toward goals.

The positive use of power and influence must focus on helping to achieve individual or team goals. It creates a desire in others in which they want to produce results — not just "what they have to."

> *"To disagree one doesn't have to be disagreeable."*
> Barry Goldwater

Expanding Your Positive Power and Influence Ability

The two essential power bases available to all leaders are expert and referent power. To maximize your ability to use these bases, consider these techniques.

EXPERT POWER

Expand expert power by implementing the model of identifying the playing field for your company.

Products and Services	People
Customers	Competition

Products/Services — Know your company products and services completely, including benefits, features, selling points, etc. Be prepared to make suggestions for improvements.

People — Know the people with whom you work. Find out about background, experience, education. Utilize their expertise as well as your own.

Customers — Know the marketplace and who are the users of your products and services. Find a way to talk to customers to get their assessments and requirements.

Competition — Know who your competitors are — what their products are and how you can gain an edge over them.

REFERENT POWER

Expand referent power by being a role model and inspiring others to want to become the leader you are.

	Be a Role Model	
Practice Peer Coaching	**Take the Initiative**	**Engage in Breakthrough Thinking**
Let your co-workers know what you think. Give both positive and constructive feedback.	Assume responsibility for follow-up. Don't hesitate to initiate action.	Go beyond incremental improvements. Look for quantum leaps.

Completing Your Influence Action Plan

Continue to work through the influence model by linking your perceptions, listening skills and power base to a specific action plan.

Identify perceptions using Active Listening
↓
Describe the situation
↓
What is your objective for changing or improving the situation?
↓
What outcomes will you achieve?
↓
What is your available base of power?
↓
How will you use your base of power in a positive way?
↓
When and where will you meet?
↓
How will you monitor progress?

CASE PROBLEM

Influence Without Authority in Developing New Products

Rick Baker became a Project Manager at PAD Corporation after several years in R&D. He knew he was hired for his technical background to shepherd new products with unique challenges through development. Baker bought into the idea of cross-functional teams, but he felt dumped into a position without real authority. He was working with people over whom he had no authority and whose bosses were making decisions that conflicted with his own. Baker wanted to get more support from his boss to run interference for him and to provide the clout Baker needed to carry out his project plans.

Baker's Recent Problems

Baker had just delivered a new product to the sales group, but the project had been fraught with problems from day one. Baker's team was staffed with representatives from R&D, engineering, finance, quality assurance, manufacturing and marketing. Each team member was expected to bring his or her own special expertise and technical insights into the development process but also were to learn about all the others' perspectives. Baker hoped to act as the pivot point and facilitator, but he found he had to push and cajole the team members every step of the way.

The project was plagued by several missed schedules, which Baker blamed on team members who gave lip service to timeframes they never intended to meet.

Baker tried to save the foundering project by becoming more directive and following up with the team members constantly. Baker believed they were not taking responsibility for their part of the project. They delayed decisions by bucking them up to their bosses. They avoided any risks and seemed most concerned with covering for themselves.

Key Questions

1. If you were Rick Baker, how would you approach fixing his problems?

2. What specific action plan and guidelines would you use to get the team back on track?

Utilize the influence action plan and guidelines to think through a framework to improve this situation.

Solution to Baker's Problem

Here are a few suggestions to help Baker get the team back on track. These ideas follow the Influence Action Plan.

1. **Understand the Situation.** First, Baker needs to discuss the situation with his boss and listen to suggestions which might encourage team participation. Baker should ask about his manager's perceptions of enlisting the support of cohort managers from functional areas. Baker will also benefit from the boss's insight as to possible barriers others may be experiencing and why. Baker also needs to determine his boss's perception of what is at stake for other managers and how to influence them.

   Second, Baker needs to talk with his team both individually and as a group. He needs to identify that he realizes the team is not operating at its highest level of performance. He should state his interest in finding out what is holding the team back from doing its best. It is important for people not to feel as if they are being blamed. Baker needs to listen and develop an appreciation for the experiences of the team. He needs to send the message that he is open to suggestions and will examine his own leadership style related to the feedback he receives.

2. **Identify Specific Issues.** Baker needs to engage members of the team in solving the problem. The team needs to make a list of all the barriers preventing peak performance. The team then sorts through information it uncovers through a variety of methods, including individual and small-group discussions, a self-report survey which it develops, possible benchmarking of a team exemplifying "Best Practices" and other modes of inquiry.

4

3. **Develop a Strategy.** Baker and the team can now develop a strategy to improve its own individual performance and that of the team as a whole. The team needs to identify a vision for success, objectives it aims to achieve and the positive outcomes it expects. The team should anticipate possible resistance and allow for some contingencies in executing the plan.

4. **Implement the Plan.** Baker needs to focus on ways he will guide the team and influence positive results. Baker should consider all the bases of power and determine what are the optimal sources of power he can use with individual team members. He should also consider talking with the team about how the team can use the bases of power to influence others in the organization.

Note: Baker's frustration appears to have developed because he wasn't clear about the concerns of this team. He blamed team members for missed deadlines and not doing their best. The more directive he became to assure timely completions, the more the team delayed the project. Therefore, the use of coercive and legitimate power would probably continue to backfire. Perhaps Baker's best strategy to influence his team to accept responsibility and achieve better results included the use of both reward and referent power.

What Do You Think?

Chapter 5 will expand your understanding of motivation and provide you with more tools that will help you "coach" Baker in achieving better results with his team.

Increasing Influence Without Authority

The need exists for leaders to increase their ability to influence employees at all levels. Some suggestions for applying influence at all levels involve a shift in the organization's work environment to encourage employees to take more responsibility.

Examples:

Current Situation	Vision	Closing the Gap
Top-down decisions	Decisions made at lowest level	Empower individual and team leaders
Limited exposure to business plans	Conduct quarterly business reviews	Begin interactive briefing for all employees
Lack of cross-functional communication	Departments are boundaryless	Create cross-functional teams at all levels

Personal Influence Exercise

1. Identify two people who influence you the most in your work. Why?

2. Identify two people who influence you least in your work. Why?

3. Who do you think you influence most?

4. Who would you like to influence most?

4. Who would you like to influence more in your work?

Utilize the learning from your personal experience to increase your ability to influence individuals and teams in your day-to-day work.

4

> *"Happiness lies in the joy of achievement and the thrill of creative effort."*
> Franklin D. Roosevelt

Summary

The ability of leaders to influence others to take action will have a dramatic effect on the results that can be achieved. Many leaders are placed in a position without formal authority or legitimate power. They must influence peers to commit to action plans and produce business results.

The Influence Increasing Model and its four steps described in this chapter provide a framework for all types of leaders to be successful in expanding their abilities to influence others. Understanding and utilizing different bases of power is another pivotal tool in influencing people to align themselves and contribute to a team vision and goal.

Questions for Personal Development

1. What is the major emphasis of this chapter?

_____

_____

_____

_____

2. What are the most important things you learned from this chapter?

_____

_____

_____

_____

3. How can you apply what you learned to your current job?

_____

_____

_____

_____

4. How will you go about making these changes?

_____

_____

_____

_____

5. How can you monitor improvement?

_____

_____

_____

_____

6. Summarize the changes you expect to see in yourself one year from now.

_____

_____

_____

_____

4

CHAPTER 5

Leadership and Motivation

5

One burning question always surfaces when a discussion about motivation begins. "Can you really motivate someone?"

Many believe that leaders can motivate others. But when you look at the essence of motivation or the willingness of individuals to expend the effort to achieve specific goals, the role of the leader becomes more clear.

The responsibility of the leader is to create an environment where individuals and teams are able to commit to action required by the mutually agreed upon goals. For a leader to help unlock the willingness in others, it is important for leaders to understand their personal motivation and how to use motivational techniques and feedback to encourage others to reach peak performance.

The idea of individual ownership is also important to note. If individuals feel a genuine sense that they "count" or can make a difference in the company's success, their motivation to achieve will be much higher.

> *"You take people as far as they will go, not as far as you would like them to go."*
> Jeannette Rankin

How Leaders Approach Motivation

For leaders to establish the environment in which individuals and teams produce their best results, it is necessary to have a good foundation in motivational concepts and techniques.

In a recent survey of employees throughout the country, one key question was asked of all participants: "When you were doing your best work, what was your leader/supervisor providing in order to support you?"

Although the respondents gave many different perspectives, the most common answers were:

- Freedom
- Challenge
- Encouragement
- Clear goals
- Resources

It is evident from this research that a leader must focus on individuals and team members and provide understanding and support. This enables people to provide their own motivation.

Motivational leaders must complete these steps to help individuals succeed:

1. Understand human needs

2. Match human needs with specific job motivators, such as career advancement through skill level, employee participation and feedback on performance

3. Utilize feedback to encourage peak performance

Understanding Human Needs Survey (Part 1)

Complete the survey by ranking from 1 (lowest) to 10 (highest) the payoffs from the job as you believe the workers in the national survey actually ranked them. (See answers later in this chapter.)

5

Payoffs from the Job	What do workers nationally want most?	What do you personally rank as most important for your job?
Recognition of good work		
Feeling "in on things"		
Help on personal problems		
Job security		
Good wages		
Interesting work		
Promotion and growth in the organization		
Loyalty to workers		
Satisfactory working conditions		
Tactful discipline		

Understanding Human Needs

What motivates or provides satisfaction for people at work? Many have attempted to answer this question, but two basic theories of motivation have been widely accepted to help leaders understand and utilize motivational concepts.

Maslow's Need Hierarchy

Abraham Maslow set out to determine what stimulates employees to produce results. He established a hierarchy of needs from lowest level to highest level of need.

> **"Don't measure yourself by what you have accomplished, but by what you should have accomplished with your ability."**
> John Wooden

Self-actualization (need to fulfill one's potential)
Self-esteem (need for self-worth)
Social (Need to belong and be affiliated with others)
Security (need to feel safe from threat)
Physiological (Need for basics — food and shelter)

Maslow believed that the lowest levels of unmet needs motivated satisfaction at that level before an individual could begin to satisfy needs at the next highest level.

As lower-level needs are met, higher-level needs then become the motivators. Only one level of need tends to motivate an individual at any one time. The lowest-level unmet need would be considered a motivator.

As the environment changes, so do the motivational needs of individuals. It is very possible for individuals to move up and down the hierarchy, based on their personal situation.

Hertzberg Two-Factor Theory

Frederick Hertzberg viewed motivation in a slightly different way. He stated that the factors which create the most dissatisfaction on the job will contribute very little to individual motivation if they are improved. Some examples of dissatisfiers include working conditions, pay and company policy. The key here is that these factors must be perceived as adequate, or they will demotivate people. On the other hand, factors that provide job satisfaction or motivate individuals include advancement, recognition and challenge. They have been termed motivators.

5

Motivators "Satisfiers"	Challenge Achievement Responsibility
	Advancement Recognition
Maintenance Factors "Dissatisfiers"	Interpersonal Relations Company Policy
	Working Conditions Job Security
	Salary

> *"A genius is not a man who was made in some other image. He is just a man driven to constructive action by a great enthusiasm. Enthusiasm feeds on challenge."*
> Dr. Wilder Penfield

Linking Maslow and Hertzberg

When comparing the Maslow Hierarchy and Hertzberg Satisfaction Model, it is easier to see the key factors which contribute to job satisfaction. The challenge of leaders is to find ways of building the satisfiers into the work system to stimulate higher-level needs.

Maslow Hierarchy		Hertzberg Satisfaction Model	
Self-actualization (need to fulfill one's potential)	→	**Motivators "Satisfiers"**	Challenge Achievement Responsibility
Self-esteem (need for self-worth)	→		Advancement Recognition
Social (Need to belong and be affiliated with others)	→	**Maintenance Factors "Dissatisfiers"**	Interpersonal Relations Company Policy
Security (need to feel safe from threat)	→		Working Conditions Job Security
Physiological (Need for basics — food and shelter)	→		Salary

118

Understanding Human Needs Survey (Part 2)

The actual results are shown in Part 2 of the survey with the responses of the workers. Compare your responses in Part 1. What do you want and how can you achieve your goals?

What Do Workers Want Most?

5

Payoffs from the Job	What the Workers Themselves Wanted as Shown in Survey
Recognition of good work	1
Feeling "in on things"	2
Help on personal problems	3
Job security	4
Good wages	5
Interesting work	6
Promotion and growth in the organization	7
Loyalty to workers	8
Satisfactory working conditions	9
Tactful discipline	10

Adapted from a survey in 1980 by Ken Kovach, George Mason University.

Key Questions:

1. How close were your responses as compared to the workers in the survey? _____

_____

_____

2. How do you differentiate between your own maintenance and motivation factors? _____

_____

_____

3. How can you gain support for getting more of your motivation factors satisfied? _____

_____

_____

4. How could you help to improve the motivation of your co-workers? _____

_____

_____

Exercise

Test Your Assumptions About People and What Motivates Them

Directions: This exercise is designed to help you better understand the assumptions you make about people and human nature. There are 10 pairs of statements. Assign a weight from 0–10 to each statement to show the relative strength of your belief in the statements in each pair. The points assigned for each pair must in each case total 10. Be as honest with yourself as you can and resist the natural tendency to respond as you would "like to think things are."

1. It's only human nature for people to do as little work as they can get away with.
   _____ (a)

   When people avoid work, it's usually because their work has been deprived of its meaning.
   _____ (b)

   10

2. If employees have access to any information they want, they tend to have better attitudes and behave more responsibly.
   _____ (c)

   If employees have access to more information than they need to do their immediate tasks, they will usually misuse it.
   _____ (d)

   10

3. One problem in asking for the ideas of employees is that their perspective is too limited for their suggestions to be of much practical value. _____ (e)

   Asking employees for their ideas broadens their perspective and results in the development of useful suggestions.
   _____ (f)

   10

4. If people don't use much imagination and ingenuity on the job, it's probably because relatively few people have much of either. _____ (g)

   Most people are imaginative and creative but do not show it because of limitations imposed by supervision and the job.
   _____ (h)

   10

5. People tend to raise their standards if they are accountable for their own behavior and for correcting their own mistakes.
   _____ (i)

   People tend to lower their standards if they are not punished for their misbehavior and mistakes.
   _____ (j)

   10

6. It's better to give people both good and bad news because most employees want the whole story, no matter how painful.
   _____ (k)

   It's better to withhold unfavorable news about business because most employees really want to hear only the good news.
   _____ (l)

   10

5

7. Because a supervisor is entitled to more respect than those below him in the organization, it weakens his prestige to admit that a subordinate was right and he was wrong.   _____ (m)

   Because people at all levels are entitled to equal respect, a supervisor's prestige is increased when he supports this principle by admitting that a subordinate was right and he was wrong.   _____ (n)
                                                                    10

8. If you give people enough money, they are less likely to be concerned with such intangibles as responsibility and recognition.   _____ (o)

   If you give people interesting and challenging work, they are less likely to complain about such things as pay and supplemental benefits. _____ (p)
                                                                    10

9. If people are allowed to set their own goals and standards of performance, they tend to set them higher than the boss would.   _____ (q)

   If people are allowed to set their own goals and standards of performance, they tend to set them lower than the boss would.   _____ (r)
                                                                    10

10. The more knowledge and freedom people have regarding their jobs, the more controls are needed to keep them in line.   _____ (s)

    The more knowledge and freedom people have regarding their jobs, fewer controls are needed to keep them in line.   _____ (t)
                                                                    10

   Score your assumptions about people utilizing the Douglas McGregor Theory X and Theory Y concepts.

   Theory X — Your general assumptions indicate that you believe most people are lazy and passive. You see them as needing to be closely supervised and controlled to get results.

Theory X Score = sum of a, d, e, g, j, l, m, o, r and s — Total = _____

   Theory Y — Your general assumptions indicate that you believe most people will take responsibility for their jobs and desire to achieve results and do excellent work.

Theory Y Score = sum of b, c, f, h, i, k, n, p, q and t — Total = _____

Test Your Assumptions About People used by permission from Organizational Dynamics, Inc., Managing for Productivity.

Implications for your emphasis on Theory Y are obvious. If leaders are going to set a climate to motivate others, the individual must have an opportunity to take responsibility for his own success. In today's work environment, the ability of individuals to improve their work process will provide motivation to perform in the current job and may create opportunities for their advancement.

If you have a high Theory-X score, you must reassess your assumptions about your co-workers. You may want to conduct a similar survey on "Understanding Human Needs" as discussed earlier in this chapter. It may help you to adjust your approach to what will really motivate your co-workers.

As an individual, team or business leader, think of ways you can improve the day-to-day work systems to increase motivation.

Three Methods to Increase Motivation

The two components of job satisfaction are mastery of the skills required to perform all the responsibilities of the job and positive affiliations at work. In order to achieve optimal results in the work environment, leaders must address the ongoing challenge of creating and sustaining a motivational work climate.

There are three methods to increase job satisfaction:

1. **Improve Work Systems**

    This requires such strategies as flexible job descriptions, creative work design to encourage cross-training and multi-skill development, ergonomics, work simplification, reengineering and such methods as JIT (Just-in-Time) management — all discussed in Chapter 6.

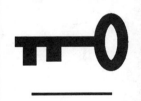

2. **Use Feedback and Coaching to Unleash Motivation in Others**

    Individualized attention to the needs and abilities of team members delivers the best chance of peak performance and a dedicated response from people to excel with job expectations. These techniques are discussed in this chapter.

3. **Increase Motivation Through Knowledge**

To satisfy the need to master the skills required in any job, it is important to recognize the need to expand abilities and learn new skills to consistently do a better job. One aspect of increasing motivation is to pay for newly acquired knowledge and capabilities. Skill-based pay systems (Pay-for-Skills Programs) are presented in this chapter.

1. Improving Work Systems as a Method to Increase Job Satisfaction

A company's core values related to partnering with employees are embedded in work systems. How keen a company is to support the training and development of employees, how worthwhile it believes certain resources are for achieving results, how well-integrated individual jobs may become to the total effort are examined through a review of a company's work systems.

"Success is more a function of consistent common sense than it is of genius."
Al Wang

• **Flexible Job Descriptions.** Designing *jobs* which expand and contract with work load, job-sharing and working from remote locations reflect some of the current orientation around how work is being done most productively. Flex time has been expanded to include flex space. Telecommuting allows employees the opportunity to interface their home computers with those at work. It reduces travel time, focuses time and space for best use by workers and saves on overhead.

In the design of *new* organizations, *jobs* actually become obsolete. There are only projects, programs, processes and competencies that are *convened* to resolve customer problems. As problems are solved, new challenges are attacked and people reconfigure as they are needed to work on the new challenges. This type of real-time orientation to work creates an atmosphere of JIT employees and utilizes what some are calling the *fishnet* organization. These concepts allow organizations the flexibility they need to move quickly into the redesign and reconfiguration of work processes and competencies to optimize time and talent in responding to marketplace demands. This is the model of today's progressive and future organizational structure and work process flow.

124

- **Work Design Which Allows Cross-Training and Multiskill Development.** Rethinking the identification of "jobs" and shifting to the concept of "work" and "job families" are gaining companies some ground as they seek to configure employee response around changing customer needs. Companies focus on how easily jobs can be "retooled" to respond to cross-divisional needs or adapted to serve a new industry. What skill sets or competency clusters align with which job families, and how best can a company equip its workforce to be adept and flexible at responding to changing customer needs?

Job compression, job enrichment and job enlargement are all parts of the same puzzle strengthening the concept that organizing work by "jobs" is obsolete. Instead, the presentation of work in terms of results to be achieved is more valuable to companies as they reconfigure the workforce for new customer challenges. Cross-training and multiskill development are inherent in building such a flexible and responsive workforce. Job-sharing is another strategy that serves both companies and individuals. It maximizes worker creativity and contribution and is one way that encourages balance in personal and professional lives. Such initiatives create opportunities for personal and professional growth as reflected by assignments with other companies to benchmark "best practices"; raising children; caring for elderly parents; taking on second and third degrees; or taking on other opportunities as people live individualized, diverse and balanced life styles. Combining job sharing and telecommuting even opens the avenue for international job exchange, where (as one example) a company and an affiliate or vendor might exchange employees. They would gain a mutual understanding of living and working in one another's cultures to expand an appreciation for such things as new markets and successful product development and launch.

5

"Leadership is complicated. It is intellectual; it is emotional; and it is physical. It is inherited and it is learned. It is the summation of the total man which must square with the myriad desires of the group."
Emery Stoops

- **Ergonomics.** Designing workspace so form follows function. Safety and productivity factors should drive everything from selection of materials and lighting to color, ventilation, security and service contracts.

- **Work Simplification/Re-engineering.** Re-engineering serves a company in streamlining work-process flow. It eliminates duplications that lead to a breakdown in integrity and cause confusion for lack of a clear focus.

- **JIT.** Evolving from continuous-improvement manufacturing processes, Just-in-Time concepts refocus a company to be driven by the customer.

Here is a long-range view of how effective work systems can increase job satisfaction and productivity. Look at suggestions for closing the gap between where you are today and the future vision.

Current Situation	Vision	Closing the Gap
• Traditional approach— boss/ subordinate	• Employees responsible for significantly improving production	• Skill development — ongoing training
• Functional organization structure (vertical)	• Fishnet organization — flexible job descriptions — job movement across departments	• More broadly defined jobs Pay for knowledge
• Partial employee involvement	• Complete employee participation at all levels	• More cross-functional teams
• Today's job	• Customer-driven work processes and projects — JIT employees	• Competency sets — transferrable skills

2. Utilizing Feedback and Coaching to Unleash Motivation in Others

- Introduction to Feedback

- Three Key Activities
  a. Recognizing Contribution — providing "positive" feedback
  b. Strengthening Performance — providing "corrective" feedback
  c. Maintaining self-esteem feedback with "I" messages

5

Introduction to Feedback

Feedback is the process of repeating back information to individuals to ensure that an objective view of the situation is held by both parties.

Feedback, when used effectively, can help individuals gain insights into their behavior and performance which can result in continuous improvement.

Key Concepts

FEEDBACK

IS	IS NOT
Descriptive	Judgmental
Specific	General
Behavior-oriented	Character-oriented
Realistic	Unrealistic
Focused on Situation	Focused on Person

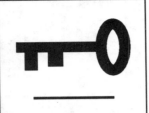

What Makes Feedback Difficult to Give and Receive?

For Managers

- They don't like making judgments and evaluations that will have serious consequences for others
- They are afraid of counterattacks or damaging the relationship they have established with the employee
- They are concerned about losing or damaging the relationship they have established with the employee
- They may feel that the employee will quit or stop performing in the areas the manager is counting on continued performance
- They don't feel comfortable in evaluating individuals who may be their technical or professional peers or superiors

For Employees

- They question whether they have the ability and/or energy to turn the situation around
- They don't understand why things are going wrong and don't want to expose their fears and concerns
- They may have had very negative experiences in past discussions and want to avoid similar situations
- They are uncomfortable discussing their performance with a manager who they do not feel is their technical equal

Action Ideas

1. Don't wait — discuss problems before they become a crisis
2. Define your view of the problem or situation before discussing it
3. Focus discussions on the problem, not the person
4. Get the employee to commit to action
5. Be accessible and supportive
6. Give regular feedback

Now let's look at three specific methods to put feedback into practice.

Recognizing Contribution (Providing Positive Feedback)

All too often, the only people who receive recognition on their work are outstanding workers and poor performers. The poor performers often get "recognition" in terms of reprimands from supervisors. The outstanding employees frequently receive recognition in terms of praise from supervisors, pay raises and promotions.

The majority of employees are neither poor performers nor outstanding workers. They meet the expectations of their jobs and their work habits seldom warrant criticism. Typically, no recognition is given to these people for the work they are doing. Yet we value their efforts and want them to continue. Recognizing contribution can even have the effect of improving performance in employees who are meeting the expectations of their jobs. The approach to giving recognition is informal, but you should carefully prepare the language you use so as not to exaggerate or create unrealistic expectations.

First, clearly describe to the employee specifically what was done to deserve recognition. The word "specifically" is important because telling an employee "you are doing a good job" doesn't let the employee know exactly what was done to deserve the compliment so he can repeat the good work. Moreover, blanket praise may inadvertently reinforce mediocre performance on the part of the employee. A second reason for making the praise specific is that it feels more sincere to the employee. Blanket praise often accompanies manipulation.

Second, express your personal appreciation to the employee. Explain **why** the employee's effort was effective, and how it positively impacted you or the work unit. The rationale behind the first two points is to let the employee know you both notice and appreciate what is being done on the job, and to ensure they know why their good effort was important.

Finally, end the conversation with a message of appreciation. This need be nothing more than saying, "Thank you."

"There are two ways of exerting one's strength: one is pushing down, the other is pulling up."
Booker T. Washington

5

Characteristics of Giving *Effective* Feedback

- Be as descriptive and non-evaluative as possible

- Focus on behaviors, not judgments

- Focus on specific things, not on individuals

- Focus on one thing at a time

- Focus on things the group or individual can do something about

- Focus on unused strengths rather than only on weaknesses

- Check with others to be sure of what was heard (clarify)

- Be gentle and empathetic

- Above all, make sure you answer the question, "Do I really want to help?" and don't give input unless the answer is YES.

- Listen with understanding (practice active listening) and be careful not to overreact

Summary

Don't!
Don't mix corrective feedback with the praise. Leave corrective feedback for a separate discussion, since corrective feedback negates any benefits from the recognition.

Do!
Practice "instant feedback" ... ideally, provide recognition immediately after the effective behavior was noticed or the contribution was made.

Recognizing Contribution

Leader

1. State clearly what the individual did that deserves comment/recognition.

2. Express your personal satisfaction with the behavior or performance. Explain why it deserves comment.

3. Again express your appreciation.

5

> ### Two Situations
>
> - Focusing on results/outcomes/milestones ("what")
>   – Recognizing contribution
>
> - Focusing on behaviors/activities/incidents ("how")
>   – "Instant" positive feedback

Receiving Positive Feedback

Employee

1. If the feedback/recognition is unspecific or vague, ask what aspect of your work or behavior was well done.

2. Express your appreciation for the feedback given.

Characteristics of Receiving Feedback

- Try to be objective and listen without interrupting

- Try not to be defensive or explain away what is being shared

- Ask for clarification and specific examples

- Feedback need not be totally valid to you. You may want to check it out with others or digest it for a while for greater understanding

- Believe everyone is telling the truth as they see it

- Don't discount positive feedback

- Summarize and feed back what you hear (practice active listening). Key here is understanding

- Not necessary to respond to every piece of data ("thanks," "ok")

Recognizing Contribution "Instant Feedback" Roulette

- Think of a co-worker who recently demonstrated effective behavior/performance
- Fill in the blanks with your own words

1. ____(Name)____, I noticed __(when/circumstance)__ that (describe effective behavior/performance).

2. I appreciate that because (why it was effective; how it helped).

3. Again, (express appreciation).

Strengthening Performance (Providing Corrective Feedback; Coaching)

How can a leader call attention to ineffective behavior or sub–standard performance in a way that is seen as constructive and supportive? It's not easy, and you're likely to arouse some defensiveness unless you handle the feedback with care. Helping people learn from their mistakes is an important management responsibility and a key element in maintaining and improving employee performance.

This five-step process will help you minimize defensiveness and turn a potentially unpleasant situation into collaborative problem-solving and positive change. The guidelines for giving corrective feedback are:

1. **Express your concern**
2. **Understand the whole story**
3. **Gain agreement that an opportunity exists**
4. **Discuss alternatives**
5. **Gain commitment and express confidence**

1. **Express your Concern**

Clear and open communication is a prerequisite to constructive feedback that leads to a solution. That's why it's important to begin the process by carefully and specifically explaining what you've observed and why you're concerned. Use "I-messages" like *"I've noticed the backlog is going up; I'm concerned about ..."* or *"I have a problem with ..."*

Avoid opening with a question or anything that may sound like a judgment or accusation. Questions like ... *"Can't you keep up with the work?"* or *"Where were you when Jim was looking for you?"* only serve to increase defensiveness and anxiety. Be tactful, but be direct. If you're too subtle, you may create misunderstanding and doubt. Remember to focus on the person's behaviors/actions and the impact/consequences of those actions, not their motives or "personality."

2. **Understand the Whole Story**

Once you've expressed your concern, immediately follow up with a question that invites explanation. For example, *"What happened? Why was it done that way? Tell me about it."* You must understand the problem thoroughly in order to solve it constructively. Listen carefully, ask clarifying questions and confirm your understanding even though you might not agree with what the person did in that situation. Use confirming phrases like, *"What you're saying is ..."* or *"Then the reason you..."* Genuine listening is a vital ingredient of both motivation and problem-solving. (Developing good listening skills was discussed in Chapter 4.)

"A leader is a dealer in hope."
Napoleon
Bonaparte

3. **Gain Agreement That an Opportunity for Improvement Exists**

After discussing the facts and "understanding the whole story," gaining agreement that an opportunity for improvement exists may be as simple as asking a "confirming" question such as, *"So, do you agree that an improvement here would help (your/the team's/the work unit's) performance?"* or *"Do you see room for improvement here also?"* Gaining agreement may be as simple as asking these questions, or it may reveal that further discussion/clarification of the problem is needed. Either way, it is an important step in the process of strengthening performance that must be completed before a person is willing to change his behavior or develop new skills.

Often, you may discover that behind poor performance was the best of intentions. If so, it's important to reinforce the good parts of the performance so that you can focus problem-solving only on the error or misjudgment. Otherwise, the person is likely to assume that both the reason and the action were inappropriate or incorrect. For example, suppose a report contained several errors because the typist thought it was more important to complete the report by a given deadline. Reinforcing the typist's concern for timeliness will help preserve this quality, while seeking solutions to the problem of accuracy.

4. **Discuss Alternatives**

Having expressed your concern, listened to the whole story and gained agreement that an opportunity exists, you can now discuss alternative ways to handle the situation the next time it occurs. This is important because it takes the pressure off past performance and looks constructively toward the future.

There are two ways to approach this step. First, if you want to draw out the other person's ideas, or if you can't think of any other alternatives of your own, ask for possible solutions. Second, if you have a suggestion yourself, or if there's only one course of action open, make your suggestion openly. Don't try to "lead" the other person to a solution you've already thought of by asking a series of questions. People are likely to become resentful of such a manipulative technique.

Here's how it might sound when you want to discuss alternatives. *"It was a tight deadline, and I appreciate the extra effort it took to get the report out on time. What can be done to reduce the number of typos and still get the work out on time?"*

> *"Great hopes make great men."*
> Thomas Fuller

5. **Gain Commitment and Express Confidence**

Before closing the situation, you should ensure that the employee is committed to making the improvements or changes discussed. If there is an opportunity to demonstrate improvement or change on a regular basis, you may want to discuss timelines or target dates.

Most importantly, you will want to ensure that the person leaves the discussion with his or her self-esteem intact. This can be accomplished by expressing your confidence in the person's ability to make the desired changes and by referring to other aspects of his or her performance/behavior that meet or exceed expectations. Several examples of self-esteem-building statements are as follows:
- I depend on you ...
- I have confidence in you ...
- I need your help ...
- What are your ideas ...?
- How would you ...?

In summary, even corrective feedback can be supportive and constructive when you follow a process of open, two-way communication and collaborative problem-solving.

Maintaining Self-Esteem

We all need to feel important and valued by others. Employees who feel good about themselves and are confident in their ability to perform their jobs are more motivated and productive. They are also typically more proactive and more committed to helping solve problems that arise in the work unit.

When providing corrective feedback or discussing developmental needs with employees, leaders often feel like they're in a dilemma: How to be honest and candid (employees need to know what they are doing well and where they can improve) without making the situation worse. The solution is not to avoid providing honest feedback but to do so while maintaining the person's self-esteem. The following tips will help you do so:

- **Focus on the behavior, not the person**
    - It is important that you criticize the behavior and not the employee in general.
    - Avoid using all-encompassing phrases like "you never ..." or "you always ..." These phrases are not behavior-specific and often put the person on the defensive.

- **Stress the positive**
    - Make it your practice to provide positive along with corrective feedback.

- **Be specific and sincere**
    - Make your comments specific, sincere and to the point. Use examples of on-the-job behavior to explain your point of view.

- **Express confidence**
    - Express confidence in the employee's abilities in general and in his capacity to improve.
    - Let him know that you trust him to make good decisions and allow him to do so whenever possible.
    - Use self-esteem-building statements like:
        - **"I depend on you ..."**
        - **"I have confidence in you ..."**
        - **"I need your help ..."**

- **Use the "I" Messages Technique**

    "I" messages are a means by which you can tell another person what his behavior is and how the behavior is affecting you with the **express intent** of getting him to change the behavior.

Three basic rules for how to send an "I" message are:

1. **Describe "specific" behavior**

    Tell the person exactly what you see, hear, etc., but do not judge and/or evaluate his behavior.

    Example: "Bill, I see that you knocked over the bookcase as you walked by and left it that way."

    Not: "Bill, you deliberately [judging] knocked over that bookcase because you are angry at me" [evaluating his reason].

2. **Express how you "feel" about it (not think)**

    Tell the person how you feel about his behaviors, your gut level reaction, e.g., frightened, angry, nervous, frustrated, proud, happy, glad, excited, etc., but not what you think about his behavior. It works best if you can share the underlying fear or threat rather than the instant anger.

    Example: "I feel frightened."

    Not: "I feel you shouldn't do that [thinking]."

3. **State the "tangible" effect**

    Tell the person how his behavior will affect you or others if it continues. Don't tell him how it may affect him; in other words, don't threaten him.

    Example: "One might trip over the bookcase and hurt oneself."

    Not: "If you don't pick it up, you're going to be in big trouble."

    Note: "I" messages should be quick and simple and not in the form of a lecture.

    Example: "You've helped me in solving my problem, and I'm happy and excited to be a part of this team and working with you."

    "I" messages must always be followed by active listening to work through any defensiveness caused by the "I" message.

3. Increasing Motivation Through Knowledge

Pay-for-Skill Programs

Pay-for-skill programs are increasing in popularity in American industry because they are providing the incentives for employees to be rewarded when they advance their skill levels and job knowledge.

Purpose

The purpose of pay-for-skills is to attract and retain successful employees and to provide a structure that encourages continued learning and growth required to support the business. The system provides a developmental path and substantial opportunity for advancement and, in return for the individual's contribution, a fair and equitable pay.

Definition

Skill-based pay is a compensation strategy for paying the person rather than the job. In skill-based pay, people are compensated for learning and using job-related skill and knowledge. Pay is commensurate with accumulation and application of skills and knowledge and not dependent on the job the person is performing at any given time.

The differences between the traditional job-based pay system and the more progressive skill-based pay are outlined below. The key motivation for workers is that through learning — and the ability to do more on the job — they are more valuable to the company. The company also gains an advantage through a more flexible workforce. The company and its employees are more interchangeable and workload/priorities can more easily be managed.

"The direction in which education starts a man will determine his future life."
Plato

138

	JOB-BASED	SKILL-BASED
PAY	Pay changes when the person changes jobs.	Pay changes when skills and knowledge are developed and certified.
ADVANCEMENT	Unclear. Associated with job change or promotion. Usually means waiting for a vacancy in another job or a position to be created.	Clear. Progression of skill blocks represents a developmental path with substantial opportunity for advancement which rests largely in the hands of the individual.
SENIORITY	Plays a large role. More "Time in Grade" assumes higher value and hence higher pay.	Plays no role. Skill and knowledge-development and application are what are important.

Implementing Skill-Based Pay Systems

Critical Needs
1. Clearly defined process to obtain certification of skill level
2. Training by certified instructors
3. Work plan: Task and objectives for each job
5. Assessment and certification

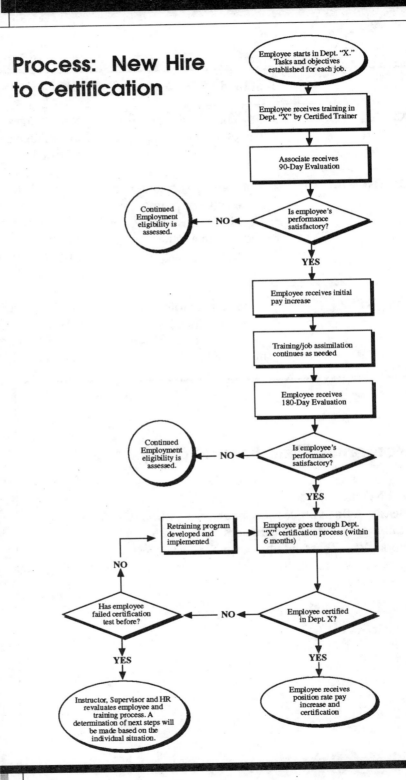

Process: New Hire to Certification

Employee starts in Dept. "X." Tasks and objectives established for each job.

Employee receives training in Dept. "X" by Certified Trainer

Associate receives 90-Day Evaluation

Is employee's performance satisfactory?

NO → Continued Employment eligibility is assessed.

YES

Employee receives initial pay increase

Training/job assimilation continues as needed

Employee receives 180-Day Evaluation

Is employee's performance satisfactory?

NO → Continued Employment eligibility is assessed.

YES

Retraining program developed and implemented → Employee goes through Dept. "X" certification process (within 6 months)

Has employee failed certification test before? ← **NO** ← Employee certified in Dept. X?

NO ↑ (to Retraining program)

YES

Instructor, Supervisor and HR reevaluates employee and training process. A determination of next steps will be made based on the individual situation.

YES

Employee receives position rate pay increase and certification

Instructor/Trainer Certification Requirements

Technical skills required:
1. Trainers must be certified in the job they will be training others in.
2. Trainers must have satisfactory or better job performance.
3. Trainers must have an excellent understanding of standard operating procedures (including safety procedures, policies and processes).
4. Trainer must be trained in how to train others.

Behavioral requirements:
1. Trainers must be positive role models.
   - Upbeat attitude
   - Proactive, always trying to make a positive contribution
   - Take initiative to make things better
   - Highest work ethics

2. Trainers must have good communication skills.
   - Fluid and conversational
   - Good listener
   - Good at asking the right questions and following up
   - Good at giving and receiving feedback

3. Trainers must be patient when working with others.

The role of the instructor/trainer

Instructors play an important role in ensuring the quality and productivity of the operation. They influence the way new and cross-training co-workers view their job and job responsibilities. As a result it is critical that the instructors be pro-active, positive and proficient.

It is desirable for those who want to become supervisors to become instructors first as part of the development process. Even if supervision is not a desired goal, becoming an instructor is a growth experience that will enhance anyone's job life.

Work Planning

Work Planning: An analysis of a job and its requirements which fortifies the key results by determining the tasks and objectives for a given period of time.

To develop an effective work plan for a job, the following should be understood:

1. What is the mission of the job, department?
2. Who are the customers, internal and external, for the job?
3. What are the customer's expectations over the next 12 months?
4. What are the customer's long-term expectations?
5. How do the customer's expectations tie into the strategic plan?
6. What personal goals does this person have?
7. Do any of the customer's expectations, the strategic plan or personal goals conflict? If so, why, and what is priority?

The end-product will be a list of key tasks and objectives which should best meet the customer's requirements and personal goals while aligning with the company's vision and mission.

Tools to Use

Task Analysis:
1. List several of the tasks that you do.
2. Determine why the task is done.
3. On a scale of 1 to 10, 10 having the most impact, determine how much impact this task has on delivering your customer's requirements.
4. On a scale of 1 to 10, 10 being the most resource-intensive, determine how much time/money/effort each task requires.

5

TASK	WHY DONE?	Impact? 1–10	Resource-intensive? 1–10	Required?

Are there any tasks that you should:
* Eliminate?
* Reduce the effort/frequency?
* Modify?
* Automate?
* Add to the current level of effort/frequency?

Setting Objectives and Measurement Criteria

Once you have answered the Work Planning questions, you are ready to define objectives and measurements of success.

Objective: A well-defined performance "target" relative to the work plan. This target is described in terms of quality, quantity, timeliness or cost. *Should be used not only to plan activities but also during the performance appraisal to evaluate work.*

Measurements: Defined criteria that establish whether objectives are successfully met.

> **A note on resources:**
> It is both futile and unproductive to set objectives that require more resources than are available. As you approach setting objectives, survey the resources needed to ensure that the objectives are appropriate and do-able.

Developing Objectives

Objectives are formed from the information gathered in Work Planning. Objectives should be mutually developed, negotiated and agreed upon. This means that throughout the process both the employee and the manager(s)/team leader(s) should establish objectives. Where there is disagreement, negotiations should take place to come to a set of objectives that are challenging, realistic and integral to performing this job. Also, objectives should be periodically reviewed and modified if necessary.

Having and using objectives offer:
* The promotion of regular discussion of job direction between the employee and the manager(s)/team leader(s).
* A mutually agreed-upon direction. Clarification of conflicts in direction (although this should happen in Work Planning for the most part).
* Self-evaluation of performance and progress.
* The focus of attention on results/outcomes.
* A good basis for performance evaluations.
* The identification of development opportunities.

144

Tips for developing good objectives are as follows:
- They should link back to business strategies and departmental plans.
- They should deal with priority expectations. Impact versus activity.
- They need to be specific.
- They should be measurable.
- They should be achievable.
- They need to be results-oriented.
- Timeframes should be established within the objective.
- Objectives should challenge and be forward-thinking — with the progress of both the employee and the company in mind.
- For each job, there should be a manageable number of objectives (about 4 to 8).
- Objectives should be well-rounded. For example, addressing quality, quantity, leadership goals, development goals, etc.

Tips for Developing Team Objectives:

- It is crucial that team objectives are mutually developed and agreed upon.
- The team leader should sit with each member to discuss how the team objectives fit with his other objectives (if applicable) to anticipate conflicts of interest or incompatible objectives.
- Team objectives should be well-communicated within the team as well as to functional areas that support the team.

Examples of Objectives
- By May 30, have the "RRR" department cross-trained, with each co-worker being cross-trained in a minimum of one other job for no less than two weeks.
- Reduce the cost of manufacturing product "A" by 5 percent by the end of the third quarter.
- To analyze the process and develop an improvement action plan for the "XYZ" process by March 1. The action plan will include resources needed, feasibility analysis and timeframes.

Examples of a Set of Objectives

1. To ensure that all safety standards are maintained by OSHA measurement standards.
2. To develop and implement a users safety manual by the 3rd quarter.
3. To select, work on and successfully implement at least one process improvement project by the end of the 4th quarter.
4. To support plant teams in measuring their safety effectiveness on a quarterly and day-to-day basis.
5. To manage the department budget within the established guidelines.
6. To provide effective coaching and assistance to colleagues yearly, situationally and periodically.
7. To practice the basic principles at all times.

Developing Measurement Systems

Well-written and developed objectives inherently define how the objective should be measured. In a system of participative objective setting, the following statements should apply to measurement.

- Individuals/Teams are held rigorously accountable.
- Measurement criteria are mutually agreed upon.
- If conditions/priorities change, objectives should be re-negotiated.

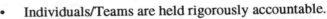

On a scale of 1 to 10, 10 being totally measurable, how measurable are your current objectives?

Assessment and Certification

Assessment is the actual evaluation of skill acquisition and application.

Certification is the administrative action which satisfies system requirements such as training records and payroll.

The purpose is to determine **with certainty** that someone has acquired and is able to apply skill and knowledge.

Assessment is a pass/fail. Either you can demonstrate the acquired skill and knowledge or you can't.

Reassessment in the case of failure may focus only on the deficiency.

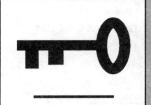

Four Methods of Assessment
- Work sample
- Demonstration
- Oral exam
- Written exam

Things to Consider

- Assessment criteria should reflect real work requirements
- The assessment should replicate actual work to the greatest extent possible
- The assessment criteria should be entirely consistent with training content
- The process must be designed to be repeatable and reliable

5

> *"Intelligence is not something possessed once for all. It is in constant process of forming, and its retention requires constant alertness in observing consequences, an open-minded will to learn and courage in readjustment."*
>
> John Dewey

Summary

Motivation requires that leaders take time to individualize each person and learn to understand his or her unique developmental and motivational needs. Motivation comes from inside a person, but a leader has keen responsibility to create a motivational work environment. From recent and substantive research in the U.S. among its major corporations, people identified several key responses they experienced in their work within motivated settings. They deserve repeating, for these are the ingredients of 21st-century companies and self-directed leadership environments: freedom, challenge, encouragement, clear goals and resources.

Three methods that have proven successful in creating motivational work environments include: improving work systems, using feedback and coaching to unleash motivation in others and increasing motivation by expanding an individual's knowledge, skills and work experience. All of these methods work toward improving an individual's self-esteem and confidence for advancing his own capabilities.

Questions for Personal Development

5

1. What is the major emphasis of this chapter?

_____

_____

_____

_____

2. What are the most important things you learned from this chapter?

_____

_____

_____

_____

3. How can you apply what you learned to your current job?

_____

_____

_____

_____

4. How will you go about making these changes?

_____

_____

_____

_____

5. How can you monitor improvement?

_____

_____

_____

_____

6. Summarize the changes you expect to see in yourself one year from now.

_____

_____

_____

_____

CHAPTER 6

Empowering Others

Empowering others has at its core the purpose of putting accountability in the hands of people who can most affect key outcomes of business success. Such areas include customer satisfaction, product and service quality and integrity, cost controls, improved vendor relationships and more. Empowering others is the key to making the **AIM Model for Leadership** a reality.

Empowering others awards them with the license and the incentive to:

- Anticipate customer needs
- Adjust products and services to become more responsive to customer requirements
- Accommodate one's own work style and behaviors to support strong internal collaboration and the integration of work-process flow
- Communicate in purposeful ways
- Celebrate successes and work continuously on process and product improvements

The business rationale for the growth of empowerment has four fundamental objectives:

1. Guarantee customer satisfaction
2. Increase market share
3. Increase profitability
4. Increase individual commitment

While it is business strategy that drives a company to empower its workforce, the impact of empowerment on productivity and morale is so strong that management is rewarded twofold for its initiatives in this regard. An empowered workforce not only achieves better performance in meeting the four business objectives but creates better work environments and more accountability to sustain them among the workforce.

The key adjustment in thinking on the part of the Top Team in achieving an empowered workforce is to shift the efforts of the organization from being *company-driven* to becoming totally *customer-driven*. This is why the shift from *control* to *commitment* happens. Workers are placed in immediate contact with the impact of their work both among themselves and with customer and vendor interface. Accountability increases geometrically along with an increased sense of responsibility and pride in one's work.

The way to achieve this shift is to empower the workforce to breathe customer satisfaction. A company must be deliberate in its strategy to empower its workforce. This cannot be a name-only process with slogans and banners. There have to be teeth in this strategy, or no one becomes empowered, and the opposite impact on productivity and morale will result.

This chapter will take you through key steps in empowering others whether your interest is as a business leader, team leader or as an individual leader of a new work process or system. Essentially you will focus on examining:

- An Empowerment Model
- A paradigm shift from an organization that is *company-driven* to one that is becoming *commitment-driven* and organized around customer needs

152

- The impact of the Empowerment Model and the paradigm shift on different leadership styles (autocratic, democratic, free-rein and blended)
- The implications of your own current situation determined through your completion of the Empowerment Readiness Assessment
- The elements of high-commitment, self-directed leadership environments
- Specific programs for empowering both the work environment and its people (e.g., management development, work systems, policies and procedures)

6

Empowerment Model

Putting strategy into action is at the core of the Empowerment Model which underlies the **AIM Leadership Model**. The operational guideline that drives the components of that model — **Action, Motivation and Influence** — is self-directed leadership. Self-directed leadership results when the company deploys authority to accompany the assumption of accountability and responsibility by individuals throughout the organization.

Empowering people throughout the organization to take on leadership initiatives appropriate to their energy, talents and expected contribution to the company requires deliberate strategy and commitment from the Top Team. The Top Team must focus on creating an environment that welcomes and sustains the kind of motivational climate in which people want to be empowered. The Empowerment Model captures the organizational link between corporate intention and individual contribution.

The Empowerment Model depicts how individuals in a company can connect their work and themselves to propel the company forward. Empowerment reflects a company's ability to move from control to commitment and to pass along authority and responsibility in step with individual skill and motivation level. People throughout the organization have a leadership role in this integrated process. Their combined responses create the forward drive of the entire company.

> *"Excellence is not an act but a babit."*
> Aristotle

The components of the Empowerment Model reflect key elements from the **AIM Leadership Model** and represent the fuel that turns strategy into action for the organization. The following represents an overview of the Empowerment Model with concrete examples of the components of the model. Also, you will be asked to reflect on your own work experience and to write down your responses in creating your path forward to an Empowerment Model in your company.

Empowerment Model

This diagram applies the concepts into an operational framework for examining the Empowerment Model.

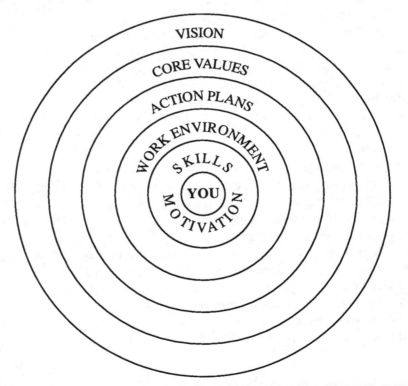

Vision

The Top Team, in tandem with other business leaders, must create a vision for the company. *Vision* serves as a vehicle for setting direction and establishing clear goals that drive everything else in the company. People from all parts of the organization take their cue from the Top Team to develop the goals and action plans that guide their contribution and work output.

Vision is often misunderstood to be an ill-defined and vague representation of a "dream" interpretation of what the company might become in the future. Rather, the company and the people that carry the company forward are better served by a vision that paints a realistic picture of what the company can become in the future.

Sample Vision Statement:

The Jefferson Group will become the leading financial services provider in the region, distinguished by the broad availability of well-defined and integrated financial products and services, as well as the knowledge, competence and customer responsiveness of our professional and dedicated people.

What is the *vision* of your company? Refer back to the vision statement you already wrote down in Chapter 3.

Core Values

The Top Team must establish leadership in the core values of the company. There may be elaborate and inclusive planning and clarifying mechanisms within the company to determine its *values*. However, unless the Top Team and those with very senior positions and formal power actually *live* the core values, they will not be real for the company.

Core values as discussed in Chapter 3 provide balance for the organization as it finds its way in the world. Values guide all relationships with clients, vendors, competitors, the industry and community at large, as well as with all the people who work for and represent the company. Values are at the heart of establishing the company's culture and work environment. They guide the rules of play and are the benchmark against which all policies, practices and decisions of the company are assessed.

> *"The quality of a person's life is in direct proportion to their commitment to excellence, regardless of their chosen field of endeavor."*
> Vince Lombardi

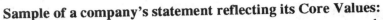

Sample of a company's statement reflecting its Core Values:

Our company is founded on our ability to serve customers by providing products and services they tell us they want. We operate under the banner of fair play and expect it in all our relationships and transactions. We commit daily to the excellence of our products and services by assuring the preparation and dedication of our employees. We expect and reward our suppliers to respond positively to our quality process and team with us in guaranteeing product integrity, reliability and the highest standards of customer service.

Does your company have such a statement? What are the Core Values of your company? List them here:

Values: _____

_____

_____

Action Plans

Action Plans are the concrete commitments and forecast results of what the company's representatives throughout all its configurations plan to do. In the Empowerment Model, people identify their individual and group goals to reflect the contributions they plan to make during the coming year's business success. Action Plans focus on such areas as improving productivity and performance, reducing and containing costs, expanding workforce capabilities and utilizing technology and other resources to a competitive advantage.

Sample Action Plan for a Team Leader:

Goal: To link team goals with company and business unit Action Plans and to align with other teams more closely in increasing market share

Objectives:
1. To improve the product development cycle and increase our speed-to-market by 20 percent in 18 months.
2. To leverage resources among ourselves and with other teams and vendors in re-engineering the product-

development cycle to achieve our speed-to-market objective and to decrease costs by 25 percent in the same time period.

3. To benchmark five other companies during the next three months that have made recent gains in improving their product-development cycles. To engage representatives from other teams in the product-development cycle in the benchmarking.

4. To train team members in the next three months in problem-solving, negotiation and creativity and to obtain the participation and partial funding for this training among other teams directly linked to the product-development cycle.

5. To expand team leadership skills in the next three months in coaching and influencing by participating in a team-leaders program and to gain acceptance and participation from other team leaders for this training.

Note: Performance-measurement goals are implicit in the objectives.

Write down your own Action Plan for yourself or your business unit, work group or team.

Goal: _____

_____

Objectives: _____

1._____

_____

2._____

_____

3._____

_____

4._____

_____

5._____

_____

6

Work Environment

Work Environment addresses all aspects of the daily operating environment which impact productivity and morale, including the physical setting, the available resources to perform work and the *climate* or work culture. The work culture includes such factors as the company's (business unit, work group and team's) values, norms ("rules of the road"), leadership styles, communication and methods for problem-solving and managing change. This is where a company provides people with encouragement, support for developing individual resources and the actual freedom to pursue new ideas and methods to advance the goals of the company.

Work Environment also represents how the company relates to employees through company policies and practices. This includes such items as medical and benefit packages, employment practices, reward systems, recognition programs, employee training and development and more.

Sample description of a Work Environment:

Our team has an incredible spirit. Members give freely to one another and genuinely care about how other people are doing, not only in their jobs, but in their lives in general. This attitude has had a tremendous impact on our productivity. The company observed our success last year and came to us to see what made us outperform our own goals. When we talked about it, we came up with these three contributing factors:

1. Our team leader was our coach, never our "boss." He never asked anything of us that he wasn't either doing himself or supporting us for doing. He was consistent and fair all the way through the year. He recognized individuals for their contributions and he held us accountable for what we promised. He made us all leaders.
2. We were united behind our goal and we committed to work together and solve problems in an atmosphere of mutual respect. The focus was on the work and not personalities. We all got training last year in teamwork.

> *"Masterpieces are not single and solitary births; they are the outcome of many years of thinking in common, of thinking by the body of the people, so that experience of the mass is behind the single voice."*
> Virginia Woolf

3. The company respected our request to supply us with new technology and access to research, without which all the team training in the world would not have given us the speed and knowledge we needed for our work.

What would you say about your Work Environment? Take notes and revisit your insights later.

_____

_____

_____

_____

_____

_____

_____

6

You

You are both the recipient and the instigator of all the Empowerment Model has to offer. The point has been made that self-directed leadership is the operational guideline of a company when it deploys authority along with accountability and responsibility throughout its environment. The individual is at the heart of empowerment. The partner relationship which a company and its employees develop together makes all the difference in whether *empowerment* becomes a reality.

The key elements to strengthen you as you expand your capabilities are your skills and motivation. You can instantly see the partnering that is required between you and the company to commit resources — time, money, energy — to developing and expanding individual capability. The partnership helps equip people with the skill base they need for meeting current and future work requirements. Similarly, motivation is a complex phenomenon that requires reciprocity, ignition and recharging all along the way.

Reciprocity or partnering is reflected in the paradigm shift in the employer-employee contract. Competitive and global markets are driving companies to shift from building and maintaining long-term and loyal employees, to enhancing the competencies and skill sets of employees while they are with the company so they are more productive on current projects and more marketable for next assignments — whether inside or outside the company. However, the most significant player in your skill development and motivation is *you*. Employees need to continually ask themselves, "What value am I contributing to the company? How can I upgrade my skills for future needs/projects?"

The following is an example of how one individual earned reciprocity from her company in developing new skills and sustaining her motivation through commitment to learning and by taking on new challenges. This scenario reflects the embodiment of the new employer-employee contract.

Julie began her service with ADTECH as an individual contributor in the graphics department. She had a two-year college degree in graphic design and was glad to begin employment five years ago with ADTECH because they were a newer company with an entrepreneurial spirit. They were focusing their marketplace advantage on technical as well as creative capabilities. Julie believed by joining the firm she would be supported in developing expanded skills in technological applications. These expectations were met early on, when Julie was able to take advantage of technological training with each new piece of equipment ADTECH acquired.

She worked diligently at all that was put in front of her. Several times she went to management with ideas that streamlined processes, saved the company money and delivered outstanding products and services to clients. Julie began servicing many of ADTECH's largest clients. Her technical ability was expanding, and now she was interested in the "business of the business." At the beginning of her third year of employment, she asked for and was awarded tuition assistance to seek a bachelor's degree in marketing. She had caught fire with expanding the business and serving clients.

No one could have predicted how well the last five years actually turned out. One of Julie's industrial clients took an interest in ADTECH because they supplied key products to several of the client's core businesses. An arrangement was struck that enabled ADTECH to acquire state-of-the-art design technology. Julie was asked to head up the new creative efforts with this technology and to link it with a customer-driven marketing approach. In five years, Julie leveraged her own capabilities and those of the company and became a key strategist, talent and leader in ADTECH's business success.

What kinds of partnering occurred between Julie and ADTECH? How did they work together over time to assure each other's success? _____

_____

_____

_____

Reflect on your own work experiences where you felt you had a strong partnership and commitment with your company.

6

Empowerment — Paradigm Shift

The following paradigm contrasts organizations that are Control-Driven with those that are Commitment-Driven. Organizations that are inward and centered on the company as a top-down organization reflect a traditional and hierarchical Control-Driven environment. Those organizations which are listening and responding to customer needs and developing their workforce to be effective in self-directed leadership demonstrate a Commitment-Driven company.

	Control-Driven	Commitment-Driven
Focus	Company	Customer
Vision	Near Horizon	Far Horizon
	Past & Present	Present & Future
Values	Given	Shared
	Top Team With Management Input	Developed With Broad Input
	Static	Revisited
Strategy	Product	Market
Leadership	Top-Down	Self-Directed
	Maintenance	Entrepreneurial
Leverage	Product	Process
Style	Hierarchical	Participatory
	Bureaucratic	Adaptive
Skills	Specialized	Broad
	Approved	Self-Propelled

Staffing	Jobs	Projects/Processes
	Work Groups	Teams
Process	Sequential	Concurrent
Communication	One-Directional	Multidirectional
	Chain-of-Command	Free-form/ Knowledge-Based
Problem-Solving	Management	Workforce
Systems	Stand-Alone	Integrated

6

Impact of Paradigm Shift on Different Leadership Styles

People have evolved as leaders in vastly different environments and most likely have learned already to find style adjustments that work best in their organizations. Effective leaders take time for assessment and seek feedback from colleagues and those whose work they direct. You may wish to review the descriptions of leadership styles outlined in Chapter 1 before considering the points here related to shifts in leadership style required for empowered environments.

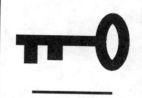

AUTOCRATIC

Autocratic leaders will find a challenge in two key ways. The key adjustment is to alter their view on the individual capabilities and capacities of workers in their companies. This type of leaders believe in McGregor's Theory X, where people are fairly limited in their work motivation and abilities. Autocratic leaders must also move toward a blended style of leadership, where they learn how to let go of control so their people can take on and master new areas of responsibility. The goal is to work in tandem with others to encourage greater autonomy so the company moves steadily toward an Empowerment Model and people become self-directed leaders.

DEMOCRATIC

Democratic or consensual leaders have developed skills useful to companies that practice empowerment. Specifically, democratic leaders usually have good communication and problem-solving skills that encourage participation. They are keen to support individual and team development. Democratic leaders sometimes have difficulty working with very independent players because they run ahead or outside the group process. The challenge for democratic leaders is to recognize how best to support the contributions of such individualists. They need to provide them with enough room to create and innovate toward the goals of the company and then link their efforts in a significant way to the work of the rest of the group. Sometimes it is effective to give these innovators specific leadership responsibility that brings them into purposeful contact with the group or team.

FREE-REIN

Free-rein leaders blend enormous skill into an empowered environment. They not only like independent and autonomous work initiatives, they expect them. The difficulty for free-rein leaders is to modify their style so manageable amounts of freedom and independence evolve in individuals in a timely and functional way that serves both the company and the person. Too much, too soon, too fast will cause people to short-circuit and perform ineffectively.

BLENDED

Leaders who have become adept at a blended leadership style know how to integrate and apply various aspects of the above leadership styles according to the maturity and experience of the people whose work they direct. Blended leaders can be tapped to serve as champions in passing on their capabilities quickly to others. In this regard, they will serve as peer mentors to other leaders and contribute to developing self-directed leadership as an intrinsic part of the work culture. The challenge here is to help the organization adjust to leadership initiative from people without formal authority over others. Those who practice a blended leadership style serve their companies as linking pins in developing leadership throughout the whole organization.

Impact of Paradigm Shift on Different Leadership Styles

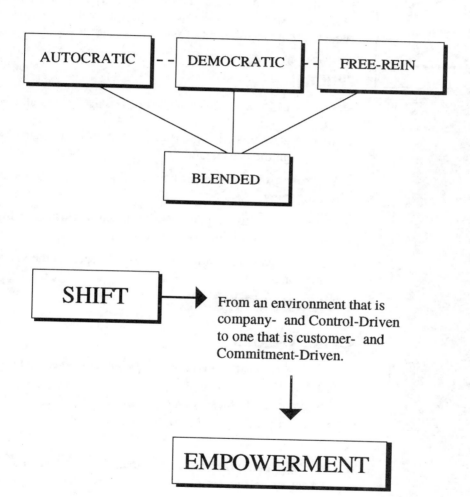

6

Exercise: Empowerment-Readiness Assessment

Complete the following **Empowerment-Readiness Assessment** to determine how far along both you and your organization are with operating in an empowered environment. Rate your answers on a scale of 1–5, with 5 representing the highest level of readiness. Then, note each score to the right of your response.

VISION

None	Somewhat	Practicing	Progressing	Accomplished
1	2	3	4	5

1. My company sets clear goals and communicates them easily throughout the organization. _____

2. My work group relates our goal-setting strategies to the goals of the company. _____

3. The vision of our company is clear because our leadership communicates it with words and actions. _____

4. Our Top Team determines and regularly revisits the vision for our company. _____

VISION TOTAL   _____

CORE VALUES

None	Somewhat	Practicing	Progressing	Accomplished
1	2	3	4	5

1. Our company has a set of Core Values that are reflected in our work, our products and how we treat our customers and one another. _____

2. Our Top Team practices our company's Core Values and serves as an example that they are not name-only concepts. _____

3. The entire company has input into creating the Core Values of the company. _____

4. We revisit our Core Values on a periodic and routine basis. _____

CORE VALUES TOTAL   _____

ACTION PLANS

None	Somewhat	Practicing	Progressing	Accomplished
1	2	3	4	5

1. My work group creates Action Plans that reflect the company's goals. _____

2. Different teams and work groups at my company share their Action Plans as they relate to shared interests or improving our work-flow process. _____

3. We use and modify our Action Plans on a continuous basis throughout the year. _____

4. Action Plans are used within my organization to empower people where authority is passed along with accountability and responsibility. _____

ACTION PLANS TOTAL _____

WORK ENVIRONMENT

None	Somewhat	Practicing	Progressing	Accomplished
1	2	3	4	5

1. The work environment at our company supports the Empowerment Model and the principles of the **AIM Leadership Model**. _____

2. Our company's policies and practices toward customers and employees reflect integrity with our values. _____

3. Leadership styles are effective and produce empowerment in our company and in my work group. _____

4. Communication and problem-solving are effective in my company. _____

WORK ENVIRONMENT TOTAL _____

6

YOU

None	Somewhat	Practicing	Progressing	Accomplished
1	2	3	4	5

1. My company provides training and appropriate resources to increase my skills to match the authority and responsibility they expect from me. _____

2. I am planning ahead to what my company may need from me in the future. _____

3. I am developing myself in more than one area because I know workers have to be very flexible and able to shift quickly to different parts of the business as needed. _____

4. I understand and am becoming skilled at self-directed leadership. _____

YOU TOTALS _____

Composite Scores

Now compile the scores you rated for the individual components of the Empowerment Readiness Assessment. This will give you an indication of where you think your company, work group and you are strong in creating and working in an empowered work environment.

AREA	SCORE
VISION	_____
CORE VALUES	_____
ACTION PLANS	_____
WORK ENVIRONMENTS	_____
YOU	_____
TOTAL	_____

Use this scale to interpret your total score to determine the overall empowerment readiness of both you and your organization.

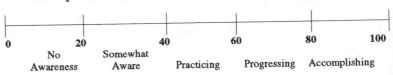

0	20	40	60	80	100
	No Awareness	Somewhat Aware	Practicing	Progressing	Accomplishing

The Elements of High-Commitment, Self-Directed Leadership Environments

To ensure that employees can accept and excel at the challenges the company entrusts to them, companies themselves must commit to following through with the Empowerment Model and process. High-commitment, self-directed leadership environments need to be strengthened continuously, as we have already examined in the Empowerment Model. The way for a company to achieve an empowered workforce is to partner at every step of the way with employees.

The company must develop a **strategy** that is driven by its **vision, mission (goals)** and **core values.** Business strategy centers on customer satisfaction, increasing market share and increasing profitability. Companies that will get the most gains will do so through committed and self-directed leaders. In order to deploy all it intends in the creation and alignment of purposeful actions plans, a company will develop and empower its workforce. The work environment needs to embody all the operating norms that make self-directed leadership capable of succeeding.

The company in its progression from **control** to **commitment** has wonderful opportunities to work in tandem with employees in **developing skills** and identifying necessary **resources** to **leverage company capability** in the marketplace. Each individual (the YOU of the Empowerment Model) has the reciprocal responsibility to determine what the company needs him or her to learn and contribute both now and in the future. In this way, each employee uses his or her motivation to meet the challenge for expanded skills. Smart companies create many work systems, policies and procedures to support, recognize and reward employees in their progressive contribution to the company.

Examine the diagram depicting the elements of a high-commitment, self-directed leadership environment. This represents a self-managing work environment that puts customers first and translates vision and values into results.

> *"The common idea that success spoils people by making them vain, egotistic and self-complacent is erroneous; on the contrary, it makes them, for the most part, humble, tolerant and kind. Failure makes people cruel and bitter."*
> W. Somerset Maugham

6

The Elements of High-Commitment, Self-Directed Leadership Environments

Re-engineering &
Quality Processes

Rewards

Merit Pay/
Incentives

Flexible Job
Description

Skill
Development

HIGH-COMMITMENT, SELF-DIRECTED LEADERSHIP (Customer-Driven)

Leadership

Employee
Involvement

Work Teams

Leadership Climate
& Styles

Creating a Self-Directed Leadership Environment

The **AIM Leadership Model** demonstrates the principles and behaviors of **Action, Influence** and **Motivation.** It positions organizations, their management and their workforces to condition and tone themselves to create and sustain high-commitment, self-directed leadership environments.

There are four major areas to address in creating and sustaining such work environments:

* Employee skills Building
* Leadership/Management Development
* Employee Influence
* Policies and Procedures

Taken together, these are the elements that translate a Top Team's vision of an empowered work culture into a motivated and entrepreneurial culture capable of recharging itself. These elements reflect the partnership agreement employees and employers are making to one another to pull them into the future.

Employee-Skills Building

The rationale for developing employees to perform in their current jobs is well documented in human resources practice and theory. Requirements to meet work expectations are often correlated to necessary skills to meet those requirements. Assessments provide gap analysis as to what skills individual employees still need in order to perform effectively in those capacities. High-commitment, self-directed leadership environments take this approach into the future.

The partnership of advancing the company, the work team and the individual's capabilities becomes part of a strategic mindset for all the organization. The increased challenges of fulfilling the needs of customers by working in today's fast-paced, technological settings place new demands on employee-skill levels and expanded areas of expertise.

Some key questions to ask yourself about developing skill sets include:

1. How long has it been since a skill-set needs assessment was done for critical work areas in your division or work group?
2. What might you do to initiate such a review process?
3. Are there baseline-competency models emerging from competitor companies?
4. What gaps exist in your work area between requirements and skills?

Leadership/Management Development

Companies committed to transcending from *control* to *commitment* are very deliberate about developing management and leadership abilities that achieve the assumption of responsibility by employees throughout the organization. They know they must delegate authority if employees will become empowered to accept accountability for results and commit themselves to solving problems as they occur.

Ensuring strong initiatives in leadership/management development is like guaranteeing one's own professional-development program. Successful and integrated strategies include plans for:

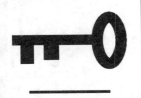

- **Determining Organizational Readiness** — assessing the current leadership/management mindset, culture, practices, training mechanisms and results.

- **Managerial-Styles Assessment** — assessing the current operational leadership/management styles and determining effectiveness and deficits for the work environment (industry) both now and in the future.

- **Team-Leader & Member Skill Development** — instituting and nudging the next tier of training for leading and contributing to teams.

172

- **Orientatior to Employee Involvement, High-Commitment & Self-Directed Leadership** — driving leadership behavior throughout the organization where responsibility for "getting the job done" is shared in creative and efficient new ways. Here people are more autonomous in their work and have access to information and resources located throughout the company.

- **Leadership/Management Steering Committee** — constituting a mentor group (with representatives from throughout the organization) who will steward the leadership/development process as it evolves and advances within the company. This is one safeguard in insuring its longevity and purposefulness. Some key questions to ask yourself about leadership/management development:

  1. **Does management reflect the company's values in their actions?**
  2. **How long has it been since your company had a leadership assessment in your work group?**
  3. **What kind of training and development programs does your company have, and what has been useful to you, your peers or team members?**
  4. **How does your company encourage, develop, recognize and reward employee participation?**

Employee Influence

As employees are asked to take on more responsibility, it is critical that their voices be heard as a method to gain input and suggestions on how to improve the business. Although this can be effective through informal day-to-day feedback and conversations, it is also valuable to create a more formal system to ensure the voice of the employee is heard. It is via this process that employees can influence how things get done.

Two-way Communication Programs. The purpose of a formal communication meeting is to provide a direct communication channel between the team members, team leader and business leaders. Meetings should be held on a weekly basis for about one hour. The agenda should focus on these key issues:

Individual
*   Training needs
*   What are the in-house and community resources to meet our needs?

Work Unit
*   Unit goals and objectives
*   Unit's progress
*   Week's progress
*   Problem-solving about work issues
*   Getting to know each other, e.g., values, philosophies, likes/ dislikes, hopes and wishes
*   Work procedures: what are the group's issues and concerns pertaining to our area, and how can we be more effective as a unit?
*   Learning exercises (communication, group effectiveness)
*   Latest trends in our field
*   Mutual expectations

Company — Personnel Policies
*   Corporate reorganizations
*   What's happening in other units (accountabilities, projects, etc.), and how do we fit in?
*   Business trends and how they affect us
*   Corporate programs and how they affect us
*   Up-to-date information on future issues, business forecasts, contemplated changes in facilities, equipment, policies and practices

Any issues, input and suggestions which must be addressed outside the team work unit should be summarized and sent to the appropriate business leader. Response should be made within 30 days.

Employee-Satisfaction Surveys. Over the years, employee satisfaction or opinion surveys have proven to be an excellent source of identifying problems, issues and suggestions for improvement. Key areas such as job/work environment, management practices, opportunities, safety and quality have produced a dialog with employees which have led to numerous high-impact improvements in the quality of work life — typically, the human resource department is the key to designing, administering and summarizing results to team and business leaders. It is then the leader's responsibility to hold open discussions.

A typical company example is:
- 1.5 percent monthly turnover
- 2.7 percent absenteeism
- 10 percent cost of errors and scrap

Net cost: $1 million

- with just 10 percent improvement through employee influence
  - −$500,000 savings
  - −direct to bottom line
  - −equivalent to over $5 million in sales

Some key questions to ask yourself about employee influence:

6

1. How can you and your team members make your voices heard?

_____

_____

2. What informal and formal methods of giving your suggestions will work at your company?

_____

_____

3. How can you enlist the support of your team leader and business leaders to initiate a method to receive your regular input on company issues and needs?

_____

_____

Policies and Procedures

Companies moving from control to commitment create policies and procedures that are responsive and flexible to accommodate the needs and values of employees. Initiatives are rooted in the partnering concept and relate to employees as committed team members in achieving the business goals of their companies.

- **Reward Systems/Merit-Pay Incentives.** Rewarding people for results — not for length of service alone or completion of only baseline objectives — are strategies employers like to provide. Setting aggressive market goals, putting in place new cost-control strategies and designing methods to improve productivity are the behaviors that are turning management heads. Leadership initiatives from typically unsolicited corners of the company or division are emerging from those companies that are rewarding performance with more imagination than position-only identification. Companies that want to get ahead will put incentives in the right places and the people who want the company to move forward will set the pace.

- **Flexible Work Schedules.** Creating flexible work schedules is one way to respond to the specific needs of a diverse workforce which has different commitments and peak time-frames of the day. This simple mechanism allows expanded coverage for the company with earlier and later hours and allows employees time to take care of other responsibilities with family, the community or their professions. It is great currency upon which a company trades for increased productivity and good morale.

- **Recognition Programs.** Empowering a workforce requires feedback in meaningful ways to support the creativity and contributions it seeks. Recognition programs underscore the commitment and dedication of people to achieve exemplary results. Companies make a mistake if they do not take the time to recognize people for the "extra" push that makes a real difference. Recognition programs can be creative and fun and need not necessarily entail substantial cost for the company.

- **Employee Assistance Program (EAP) and Family and Medical Leave (FMLA).** Modern life can sometimes place stressful demands on individuals and families. An extended illness of a child, a relocation of an aging parent into a supervised senior-living situation, divorce or death may make it necessary for individuals to need counseling through an EAP program or take some time off through a family-leave policy. Under the FMLA, all active employees with at least one year of service are entitled to take time off for their own serious health condition or to care for a family member with a serious health condition. They can take this time off on an "intermittent" basis; e.g., an employee who asks the supervisor on Tuesday if he can take off next Friday afternoon to place his mother in a nursing home is entitled to take that time off under FMLA. Even if the employee does not request an FMLA leave or even mention FMLA, the employee is entitled to the time off under FMLA, and the time off is treated as FMLA leave under the law. The employer is legally responsible for communicating to the employee his rights under FMLA when the employee asks for the time off.

Some key questions to ask yourself about your company's policies and procedures:

1. Do your current employee policies and practices support the best from each employee?

2. Do your policies and practices unfairly isolate and penalize an entire cluster of your employees?

3. What innovations and results are being evaluated by other companies?

4. How long has it been since you asked your employees how you can be more responsive to their needs?

177

Summary

The Empowerment Model demonstrates a process companies can utilize to create high-commitment, self-directed leadership environments. In order to achieve such dedication and commitment from employees, a company must move its own culture and operating environment from one that is company- and control-driven to one that is customer- and commitment-driven. The company must deploy authority throughout the organization in step with the accountability and responsibility people accept.

In creating and sustaining such collaborative and results-oriented environments, there is a special focus for the three types of leaders which were identified in Chapter 2. The three types of leaders impact leadership in the following ways:

1. **Business Leaders** affect change and create the conditions which guide the development of high-commitment environments. Along with top management, they create strategy, vision and live the values of the company.

2. **Team Leaders** align their team members with the business strategy, vision and values of the company. They coach team members to develop action plans that link with those of the company.

3. **Individual Leaders** develop skills and influence those around them. Business results through their own self-directed leadership in key areas of responsibility.

Questions for Personal Development

1. What is the major emphasis of this chapter?

_____

_____

_____

_____

2. What are the most important things you learned from this chapter?

_____

_____

_____

_____

3. How can you apply what you learned to your current job?

_____

_____

_____

_____

4. How will you go about making these changes?

_____

_____

_____

_____

5. How can you monitor improvement?

_____

_____

_____

_____

6. Summarize the changes you expect to see in yourself one year from now.

_____

_____

_____

CHAPTER 7

Developing the Leader in You

Introduction

For leaders to develop at every level of the organization, their commitment to learning and growing in leadership ability is mandatory.

As explained in the **AIM Leadership Model**, leaders must use a planned approach to guide others to action through influence, motivation and empowerment. To achieve significant results, leaders must frequently assess their skill levels and be prepared to improve their skills on a regular basis.

The foundation of strong development is to have a clear set of skills to work toward. In addition, an assessment process to help identify skills which need strengthening will provide the springboard for launching the leaders of the future.

Fundamentals of Leader Development

Every employee in the organization has an opportunity to develop leadership skills. The very foundation of the learning process is to understand that development of skills is personal-growth-oriented. Simply, this means that you are continuously building on the knowledge, skills and abilities that you currently possess.

> *"One is on the way to being useless when he stops learning."*
> Ruth Smeltzer

Think of your leadership development as an acquisition of knowledge and skills which will improve your ability to achieve results with others.

These four fundamentals will help to set the stage for your personal development.

Fundamental 1 — Principles of Leadership Development
- You must assume responsibility for your development.
- You must develop "mirrors" in your organization to provide feedback on your current skill level.
- You must prepare a personal development plan to initiate development activities.

Fundamental 2 — Personal Awareness
For development to be successful, you must recognize that making an acquisition of knowledge and skill is necessary to achieve results in your organization.

Fundamental 3 — Ownership
You must understand that no one can do it "to you or for you." You must commit to undertaking the educational activities necessary to grow and develop. This may mean some personal sacrifice and time commitment to ensure success.

Fundamental 4 — Learn by Doing
The amount of formal classroom time available for your development will be limited. You must be willing to try out your knowledge and skill acquisition on the job. This will mean making a conscious effort to try new ideas while you are performing your job.

The Stages of Development

Recognition   The individual must recognize that making a change in behavior or developing new skills will be beneficial or is necessary.

Choice   The individual must make a free-will decision to do something about the opportunity to improve or to develop new skills that he has recognized.

Plan/Act   The individual must think through what is needed to make the change and develop a specific, systematic approach.

Support   The understanding and assistance of others is usually helpful and often necessary, in order to carry out the plan and overcome obstacles.

Development Partnerships

The success of any development process is very dependent on how well the individuals, team leaders and business leaders are willing to provide support and direction.

Employee	Team Leader	Business Leader
Establishes interests/ goals	Creates a positive climate — trust	Provides principles/ strategies for development
Seeks feedback/ advice	Gives candid feedback	Provides an investment
Provides motivation/ effort	Is a coach, not a boss	Training and development opportunities
Is realistic	Is a role model	Career-path information
Takes ownership Is proactive	Is an advocate	

Leadership Focus Increases as Business Leaders Develop

The transition from individual leader to team leader and eventually to business leader requires a shift in focus. The individual leader will spend most of the time applying his core knowledge and skill obtained during his technical-education process. An example would be a company specialist who would work primarily on design or problem-solving. This individual would be responsible for his own work but would often work with a team of peers.

The team leader is responsible for the output of a group of individuals, either reporting directly or indirectly. The team leader is focused on guiding that team to the required actions but often must use interpersonal skills, influence skills and collaboration to motivate the team to achieve results. The focus of the team leader is a balance of technical and relational abilities.

The business leader is most likely responsible for a business unit or department. This individual may have several team leaders who report indirectly. The focus of the business leader is much more on business strategy and people than on technical depth of knowledge and skill.

Developing Your Leadership Ability

To acquire the knowledge and skill you will need to grow in leadership ability, the following are essential:

1. A set of core leadership knowledge and skills or competencies.
2. A process for assessing your current skill level.
3. A guide to personal development.
4. A method to test your assessment.

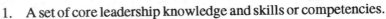

Core Leadership Competencies Inventory

The list of skills that leaders are expected to develop can be very extensive. The goal of the core leadership competencies inventory is to provide a focus for your development as a leader. The ten core skills will help you to establish a basic foundation and implement the **AIM Leadership Model**.

- Communication
- Personal impact/influence
- Drive for results
- Problem-solving/decision-making
- Team leadership
- Flexibility — Respond to change
- Breakthrough thinking
- Empowerment
- Values orientation
- Technical expertise

Progression of Knowledge and Skill for Leaders

Knowledge/ Skill	Individual Leader	Team Leader	Business Leader
Communication	A S	S FD	FD
Personal Impact/ Influence	A	S	FD
Drive for Results	A	S FD	FD
Problem-Solving/ Decision-Making	A	S	FD
Team Leadership	A	S	FD
Flexibility	A S	S	FD
Breakthrough Thinking	A	S	FD
Empowerment	A	A S	FD
Values Orientation	A	A S	FD
Technical Expertise	A S	FD	S

KEY: A   Awareness — Possess the basic skills and knowledge to do the job.
        S   Skillful — Is able to demonstrate most aspects of the skill
        FD   Fully Developed — Is able to demonstrate all aspects of the skill on a regular basis

Evaluating Your Leadership Competencies

Skill Assessment

Assess your current skill level by reviewing the definition of each skill and then assigning your level of competence.

A = Aware

S = Skilled

FD = Fully Developed

Keep in mind the shading chart, which will help you to identify the skills and competence for your leadership level in the company.

Complete the Assessment

Check your current level

- Individual leader
- Team leader
- Business leader

Next check your current level of competency. Look for opportunities to improve.

Skill	Definition
Communication Skills	Structures and communicates material effectively in both written and oral forms, including group presentations. Able to clearly articulate and present ideas, concepts and suggestions to others. Also includes listening well to others' points of view by demonstrating attention and conveying understanding.

Important Considerations

- Do you understand how to use the appropriate communication channels — telephone, memo, e-mail, face-to-face?
- Have you received feedback on your written or verbal skills?
- Do you take advantage of every interaction as a learning experience?

Assess Competency Level

A	S	FD	Is there opportunity to improve?

7

Skill	Definition
Personal Impact/ Influence	Demonstrates the ability to quickly gain attention and respect from others, including peers, cross-functional groups, superiors and subordinates. Is quickly perceived by others as a credible and valuable source apart from formal position or authority. Can move others to commit to a course of action and constructively influence them to accomplish tasks or reach objectives. Makes a difference in any projects that are undertaken.

Important Considerations
- Do you use a planned approach to influence others?
- Are you aware of how you are perceived, with respect to credibility?
- Are you consistently able to help your team move to achieve its objectives?

Assess Competency Level

A	S	FD	Is there opportunity to improve?

Skill	Definition
Drive for Results	Demonstrates a bias for action, for trying new ideas and for getting tasks done. Sets high standards of accomplishment for self and others. Pursues business objectives with a sense of urgency. Demonstrates a willingness to take initiative and go beyond the minimum requirements of effort/activity. Consistently accomplishes goals.

Important Considerations
- Do you have a vision?
- Are your plans aligned with business objectives? Do you have specific measurements in your work?
- Are you consistently looking to perform value-added work and eliminating unnecessary tasks?

Assess Competency Level

A	S	FD	Is there opportunity to improve?

Skill	Definition
Problem-Solving/ Decision-Making	Demonstrates the ability to analyze and solve complex problems. Deals effectively with large amounts of data, changing conditions, incomplete data or uncertainty. Recognizes how seemingly unrelated issues or events interact and affect one another. Gets to the essence of complex problems quickly and generates effective courses of action. Is able to identify critical information from a wide range of data and use it to make effective decisions. Accurately interprets and understands quantitative and/or financial data.

Important Considerations

- Do you have a problem-solving methodology? Are you able to quickly identify problems?
- Are you decisive? Do you act on information quickly? Do you find ways to gather input on your assumptions so as not to operate in a vacuum?
- Are you clear on your impact on the company financials, bottom line, etc?

Assess Competency Level

A	S	FD	Is there opportunity to improve?

7

Skill	Definition
Team Leadership	Achieves results by motivating and inspiring a winning team or work group. Establishes and communicates a vision and future direction for one's work unit. Sets challenging standards of achievement. Articulates improvement opportunities in a way that builds commitment to common goals and energizes others to seek and implement solutions. Helps team/ work unit overcome "pain" of change. Creates a work environment characterized by participation/involvement and continuous learning/ improvement, where individuals collectively achieve their highest potential. (Applies also in situations where formal reporting relationships with team members do not exist, such as cross-functional teams.)

Important Considerations

- Are you able to focus your team on common goals? Have you received feedback on your leadership skills?
- Are you able to align resources necessary for the team to succeed?
- Have you focused the team on building strong relationships to help accomplish its goals?

Assess Competency Level

A	S	FD	Is there opportunity to improve?

190

Skill	Definition
Flexibility/ Responds to Change	Demonstrates the ability to establish priorities and implement actions in changing, unclear or ambiguous situations. Makes effective decisions without the benefit of complete data/information. Can effectively alter course of action or style of management when warranted by new or changing circumstances. Is resourceful. Demonstrates the ability and willingness to adopt the role of leader/manager or team member/contributor, depending on the task at hand. Able to work effectively outside formal lines of authority.

Important Considerations

- Do you have a clear understanding of how to manage change, including dealing with resistance?
- Are you able to quickly shift priorities without losing focus?
- Have you had the opportunity to assume a lead role on a project? Were you able to do whatever it takes to get the job done?

Assess Competency Level

A	S	FD	Is there opportunity to improve?

Skill	Definition
Breakthrough Thinking	Generates new ideas and insights. Suggests new approaches and enjoys opportunities to "play" with and "brainstorm" ways to improve systems and tasks. Can see an idea through from concept to reality. Is focused on making "quantum leaps" in productivity, not just incremental improvements.

Important Considerations

- Are you comfortable in thinking "out of the box?" Are you able to break old paradigms in your approach to problem-solving?
- Do you know the industry's best practices for your work?
- Can you take a creative idea and implement it while dealing with other input?

Assess Competency Level

A	S	FD	Is there opportunity to improve?

7

7

Skill	Definition
Empowerment	Establishes clear direction and sets challenging but achievable goals. Delegates responsibility/authority commensurate with individual abilities. Provides frequent performance feedback, both positive and corrective. Effectively coaches to improve current performance and empowers people to take full responsibility for their work. Selects and develops highly talented people.

Important Considerations
- Do you understand the basic motivation concepts of Maslow and Hertzberg?
- Do you understand how empowerment can work for individuals and teams?
- Are you comfortable in giving feedback to peers, subordinates and/or team members?

Assess Competency Level

A	S	FD	Is there opportunity to improve?

Skill	Definition
Values Orientation	Understands company values and uses these values to influence individual and team behavior. Is committed to company vision and is willing to make personal sacrifices to help achieve the vision.

Important Considerations
- Are you aware of your company values?
- Are you aware of your own personal values?
- Do you make an effort to allow values to guide your behavior?

Assess Competency Level

A	S	FD	Is there opportunity to improve?

192

Skill	Definition
Technical Competence	Demonstrates expert knowledge/understanding of main technical area. Keeps abreast of new developments in his field and imparts new ideas/technologies that have a positive impact on the business or work unit. Is sought after by others for technical advice. Demonstrates comprehensive command over the technology of his area of expertise.

Important Considerations
- Do you have a method for continuing education?
- Do you have an updated list of your job requirements?
- Do you have personal goals for each business year?

Assess Competency Level

A	S	FD	Is there opportunity to improve?

Testing the Accuracy of Your Personal Assessment

After you have completed your personal assessment, you have an indication of how you feel about your level of leadership competence. But this is only part of the complete picture.

It is not unusual for individuals to rate themselves higher or lower than their current level of competence. Who can help to balance this picture and help add a degree of accuracy?

- **Peers** — These are your co-workers who work in your department, on your team or in other departments with whom you work closely.
- **Subordinates or Team Members** — These are individuals who report directly to you or team members who report indirectly to you. This group will be omitted for individual leaders.

193

7

- **Immediate Boss** — This is the person to whom you directly report. This person completes your performance appraisal.

The combination of this input is called 360° feedback.

Gathering Feedback and Information

There are two main methods of gathering feedback and information from your peers, team members and immediate boss.

1. **Active listening** is the feedback obtained from face-to-face or telephone conversations. These discussions should focus on how well you have modeled the 10 leadership skills. Include clients and customers also.

2. **Questionnaire** information is the response obtained from a written survey. This questionnaire is normally completed anonymously with the rater identifying himself as peer, subordinate or team member. This method tends to be more objective because the respondent is not identified.

Helping to Reveal Your Blind Spots

It is often most difficult to identify one's own strengths and weaknesses. The rise in value of 360° feedback systems represents the growing belief that how others see us has something to do with the total understanding of the impact a leader is having upon others.

The Johari Window was developed by Joseph Luft and Harry Ingham in 1969. This four-quadrant model shows that you may be able to uncover your blind spots and develop potential in new skill areas through the 360° feedback process.

A blind spot will be recognized when your boss, peers and direct reports all agree on a weakness which you may feel is a fully developed skill. When blind spots are identified, you should use the "Quick Tips" section to help plan improvements.

Brief Summary of the Johari Awareness Model*

The four quadrants represent the total person in relation to other persons. The basis for division into quadrants is awareness of behavior, feelings and motivation. Sometimes awareness is shared, sometimes not. An act, a feeling or a motive is assigned to a particular quadrant based on who knows about it. As awareness changes, the quadrant to which the psychological state is assigned changes. Each quadrant is defined:

1. Quadrant 1, the open arena, refers to behavior, feelings and motivation known to self and to others.
2. Quadrant 2, the blind spot, refers to behavior, feelings and motivation known to others but not to self.
3. Quadrant 3, the hidden mask, refers to behavior, feelings and motivation known to self but not to others.
4. Quadrant 4, the unknown potential, refers to behavior, feelings and motivation known neither to self nor to others.

7

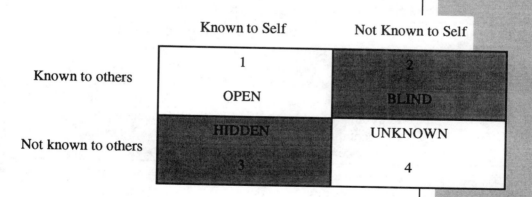

	Known to Self	Not Known to Self
Known to others	1 OPEN	2 BLIND
Not known to others	HIDDEN 3	UNKNOWN 4

*Organizational Dynamics, Inc., Managing for Productivity Program.

Organization Feedback Survey

Name of Person Being Rated _____

Rater

Peer _____

Subordinate _____

Team Member _____

*Immediate Boss_____

Please rate this individual on their leadership skills.

Rating =   **A** (Awareness) — Possesses the basic skill and knowledge

S (Skillful) — Demonstrates most aspects of the skill

FD (Fully Developed) — Demonstrates all aspects of the skill on a regular basis

Skill Area	Definition	Rating
1. Communication	Structures and communicates material effectively in both written and oral forms, including group presentations. Able to clearly articulate and present ideas, concepts and suggestions to others. Also includes listening well to others' points of view by demonstrating attention and conveying understanding.	
2. Personal Impact/ Influence	Demonstrates the ability to quickly gain attention and respect from others including peers, cross-functional groups, superiors and subordinates. Is quickly perceived by others as a credible and valuable source apart from formal position or authority. Can move others to commit to a course of action and constructively influence them to accomplish tasks or reach objectives. Makes a difference in any projects that are undertaken.	
3. Drive for Results	Demonstrates a bias for action, for trying new ideas and for getting tasks done. Sets high standards of accomplishment for self and others. Pursues business objectives with a sense of urgency. Demonstrates a willingness to take initiative and go beyond the minimum requirements of effort/activity. Consistently accomplishes goals.	

*Feedback from your immediate boss should be obtained in a face-to-face meeting.

4. Problem-Solving/Decision-Making	Demonstrates the ability to analyze and solve complex problems. Deals effectively with large amounts of data, changing conditions, incomplete data or uncertainty. Recognizes how seemingly unrelated issues or events interact and affect one another. Gets to the essence of complex problems quickly and generates effective courses of action. Is able to identify critical information from a wide range of data and use it to make effective decisions. Accurately interprets and understands quantitative and/or financial data.	
5. Team Leadership	Achieves results by motivating and inspiring a winning team or work group. Establishes and communicates a vision and future direction for one's work unit. Sets challenging standards of achievement. Articulates improvement opportunities in a way that builds commitment to common goals and energizes others to seek and implement solutions. Helps team/work unit overcome "pain" of change. Creates a work environment characterized by participation/involvement and continuous learning/ improvement, where individuals collectively achieve their highest potential. (Applies also in situations where formal reporting relationships with team members do not exist, such as cross-functional teams.)	
6. Flexibility	Demonstrates the ability to establish priorities and implement actions in changing, unclear or ambiguous situations. Makes effective decisions without the benefit of complete data/ information. Can effectively alter course of action or style of management when warranted by new or changing circumstances. Is resourceful. Demonstrates the ability and willingness to adopt the role of leader/manager or team member/ contributor, depending on the task at hand. Able to work effectively outside formal lines of authority.	
7. Breakthrough Thinking	Generates new ideas and insights. Suggests new approaches and enjoys opportunities to "play" with and "brainstorm" ways to improve systems and tasks. Can see an idea through from concept to reality. Is focused on making "quantum leaps" in productivity, not just incremental improvements.	

7

8. Empowerment	Establishes clear direction and sets challenging but achievable goals. Delegates responsibility/authority commensurate with individual abilities. Provides frequent performance feedback, both positive and corrective. Effectively coaches to improve current performance and empowers people to take full responsibility for their work. Selects and develops highly talented people.	
9. Values Orientation	Understands company values and uses these values to influence individual and team behavior. Is committed to company vision and is willing to make personal sacrifices to help achieve the vision.	
10. Technical Expertise	Demonstrates expert knowledge/understanding of main technical area. Keeps abreast of new developments in his field and imparts new ideas/technologies that have a positive impact on the business or work unit. Is sought after by others for technical advice. Demonstrates comprehensive command over the technology of his area of expertise.	

Comments:

360° Feedback — Closing the Loop: How to Make It Work for You

1. **Use Mirrors**
   Ask somebody close to you to give you continuous feedback on your progress in the areas you want to address.

2. **Dig into Your Feedback**
   - Understand it
   - Decide if it is valid
   - Select the areas you want to address
   - Put a plan together that will work for you

3. Utilize the tips for developing your leadership competence in the last section of this chapter.

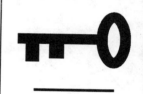

Building Leadership Competencies

Tips for Developing Your Core Leadership Skills

Take advantage of the many opportunities for upgrading your leadership skills. Utilize the input from your self-assessment and organizational feedback to pinpoint improvement areas.

Also utilize the "quick tips" list that follows to build on-the-job activities to help your leadership growth.

199

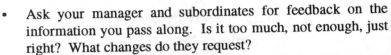

Quick Tip List

Communication Skills

- Ask your manager and subordinates for feedback on the information you pass along. Is it too much, not enough, just right? What changes do they request?
- Always work in this order: "hear, understand, interpret, respond." Don't jump from "hear" to "respond" without making sure you understand and have interpreted properly.
- Avoid interrupting people until they have finished making their points.
- Ask open-ended questions to draw out a person's thoughts and feelings by using phrases beginning with what, how, why, describe, explain, etc. "How would you do this?" or "Describe why you don't like the plans."
- Paraphrase questions you are asked to be certain of the meaning and to give yourself time to think.
- Become sufficiently familiar with the subject matter you are presenting so that you have full command of the material.
- Before making a formal presentation, anticipate and prepare for doubts and questions.
- Tailor the tone of your presentation (formal, informal, facts, big picture) for each particular audience.
- Use staff meetings, business reviews, visitor tours, or employee orientations as opportunities to practice your presentation skills.
- To polish your presentation skills, take a seminar with videotaped feedback.
- When writing, consider the people in your audience. What do they know? What can you tell them?
- Outline your memos and letters before beginning to write.
- Whenever possible, limit letters or memos to one page.
- When writing reports, summarize key points or conclusions on the first page and document them with more information on subsequent pages.
- Write a first draft of a report, then edit it. Ask someone whose judgment you respect to critique it.
- When writing for a non-technical audience, have a non-technical person (such as a spouse or a secretary) identify jargon. Then either eliminate it or include a glossary defining the terms.

Personal Impact/Influence

- In meetings and conversations, try to take a stand on key issues.
- If you are confident of your point of view, phrase your position unequivocally; avoid words that hedge (e.g., "maybe," "well perhaps," "yes, but").
- When appropriate, challenge the status quo by suggesting a new direction or innovative approach for handling a situation.
- When you make a mistake, admit it; don't defend your actions. Focus on what steps you can take to avoid the problem in the future.
- When you have to make a decision that adversely affects people, explain your rationale as clearly as possible.
- Look for an opportunity to work on or lead special projects.
- Propose a course of action on an issue that will have important impact on your department/organization.
- If you are confident of your position, don't be afraid to show emotion or be dramatic when you speak. Don't qualify or dilute your position.
- Ask your manager to specifically identify blind spots in your leadership ability or the manner in which you make an impact on people.
- Adopt a "can do" attitude and approach challenges from a problem-solving perspective. Look for alternative solutions rather than why things can't be done.
- Become quicker to offer your ideas in a group setting, especially as a subordinate, rather than sit back and wait for others.
- Initiate new ideas, objectives and projects with your superior and with your subordinates.
- Attend a training seminar on personal style, presentation and influence.

Drive for Results

- Make a daily "to do" list. Prioritize each task.
- Schedule regular meetings with your management to review their priorities so you can clarify your goals and objectives.
- Analyze goals that have worked against you in the past to pinpoint where you have miscalculated in terms of timing or tasks. Determine if there is a pattern to your miscalculations and construct a plan to avoid these pitfalls in the future.

- When establishing goals and objectives, work backwards from the desired result to plan the action steps that are required to produce it.
- In establishing a goal or objective, quantify the time frame and the desired result.
- Examine your pattern of delegation. Could you delegate more and refocus your efforts to get more accomplished?
- Be committed to deadlines you set even if others seem flexible.
- Ask your manager to specifically identify situations where you were not sufficiently goal-focused.
- If you find it difficult to maintain a high energy level on the job, assess your fitness level, giving consideration to nutrition, exercise and sleeping patterns.
- Make some form of public commitment to your goals so others will encourage you to reach them.
- Ask to work on a project that is important to the department, has high visibility and will require hard work.
- Utilize your "peak" energy periods to complete difficult or complex tasks; use your "valleys" to do repetitive or fast turn-around tasks.
- Deliver on commitments; recognize that sometimes delivering a result takes precedence over perfection.
- Attend a time-management seminar.

Problem-Solving/Decision-Making

- Detail the specific causes of a problem before selecting a solution. When appropriate, involve others in the process to gain different perspectives on the situation.
- Use brainstorming to develop several alternative solutions to a problem.
- Construct a tentative action plan for solving a problem. Ask your manager or someone you respect to critique your plan.
- Play "Devil's Advocate" with the solution you develop for handling a problem.
- Ask to work with someone you believe has outstanding analytical and/or problem-solving skills. Take note of their techniques and habits.
- Use local experts to help solve specialized problems such as mechanical, medical, etc.

- To broaden a possibly narrow process of problem analysis, analyze a situation from the perspective of different departments, managers or work units. Review the viewpoints with your manager.
- Practice analyzing work unit or company budgets/financial reports. Review your analysis with a knowledgeable manager.
- Seek input from subordinates, and have subordinates participate in problem-solving and planning activities.
- Go to your boss with your analysis and a recommended solution rather than with a problem alone.
- Attend an appropriate training course to build analytical skills in a particular area (e.g., financial, statistical, etc.).
- In analyzing a situation, list the specific organizational issues, politics and personality issues which must be considered.
- List the assumptions that you are making about a situation before jumping to a conclusion.
- Always consider a worst-case scenario; make contingency plans based on this premise.
- List the key players who are directly or indirectly affected by a situation.
- Ask others for their evaluation of a situation or issue. Then ask them to critique the potential solution you have developed.
- Identify an ideal solution to a problem. Then work backwards to develop a practical strategy for handling the situation.
- Explain the facts of a situation to someone whose judgment you respect, and ask how they see the situation.
- Develop several alternative courses of action. Prioritize the alternatives in terms of feasibility, practicality and appropriateness of result.
- Assess several decisions you have made over the past six months. Identify specific strengths and weaknesses in your approach. Determine if there is a pattern to issues you miss. Construct a plan that capitalizes on your strengths and eliminates your weaknesses.
- Weigh the pluses and minuses of a decision by outlining the potential business, people and organizational consequences.

7

Team Leadership

- Develop and communicate an overall direction or "mission" for your work unit. Make sure you communicate how your employees' work fits into broader company goals.
- Establish a "group identity" and work at building pride in group membership — "esprit de corps."
- When delegating assignments, provide the bigger picture of "why" the assignment is important in addition to advice on "how" it might be accomplished.
- Recognize that, depending on their maturity, subordinates will require different leadership styles on different tasks.
- Spend more time face-to-face with subordinates finding out how they are doing both professionally and personally.
- Once you make an assignment, give employees freedom to deliver the results using their methods. Build in regular progress points to ensure the final result.
- When delegating an assignment, be certain you also delegate appropriate authority. However, never delegate final accountability.
- Involve employees in the goal-setting process; this increases their commitment to delivering the result.
- Praise people in public; criticize them in private.
- Determine three steps you can take that will communicate to your people that their efforts are meaningful.
- When disagreements erupt between individuals, re-emphasize the broader goals and look for common ground which may link both sides of the issue.
- Encourage creativity among subordinates by keeping an open mind to their suggestions and avoiding words or behaviors that tend to stifle or inhibit the free flow of ideas.
- Attend a training seminar focusing on leadership that provides "upward" feedback from subordinates.

Flexibility

- Develop your comfort level with being an individual leader as well as a team leader.
- Seek other opinions and input prior to making a decision.
- Utilize active listening to get the whole story.
- Be prepared to incorporate suggestions into your decision-making process.

- Develop ability to deal with ambiguity in situations without clear guidelines.
- Expect changes — be prepared to change direction if your leadership or situation requires it.
- Think about lateral movement to learn new skills.
- Anticipate change — welcome change as an opportunity to learn and grow.
- Take the initiative to learn new skills to use in your current job and in a future assignment.

Breakthrough Thinking

- Restate a problem/situation from several different perspectives (e.g., How would the *client* see it).
- Use group brainstorming techniques to generate innovative or creative strategies for approaching particular situations.
- Ask resources outside the company (e.g., vendors, consultants, professional colleagues) if they have come across an innovative method of handling a situation.
- Keep abreast of new and innovative approaches to work by reading technical and business journals on a regular basis.
- Attend professional meetings and conventions to keep abreast of creative or innovative approaches to work.
- Use a staff meeting to brainstorm new approaches for difficult or recurring problems.
- Once a quarter, focus on a system or procedure that is well accepted. Sit back and critique it. Develop a new approach for handling it.
- Ask to work on an assignment with someone who you consider to be innovative and creative. Take note of his techniques.
- Talk about the situation with someone from a different discipline, management level or perspective.
- Practice coming up with what may at first seem like "dumb" and way-out ideas to get your creative juices flowing and reduce your self-criticisms.
- When considering alternatives, ask yourself and others, "Why not?" instead of, "Why?"

7

Empowerment

- Identify responsibilities you are personally handling that would be developmental for each of your subordinates and delegate accordingly.
- If a delegated assignment is not up to your expectation, do not redo it yourself. Coach your employee on what needs to be changed and have them rework it.
- Utilize teams of strong and weaker employees to handle assignments. If you always hide your weaker people, they will never have the opportunity to improve.
- Use rotational assignments or cross-training to broaden an employee's skill base.
- Provide employees with project- or task-force leadership opportunities.
- Provide people with timely and accurate performance feedback, particularly when they are not performing up to your expectations.
- Make a list of the tasks or projects assigned to your people to determine if you are spreading the workload and challenging projects fairly.
- Assign some tasks to each employee which stretches their abilities.
- Assign an experienced or "expert" employee to work with or act as a mentor for another employee.
- Attend a training seminar focusing on leadership and people management.
- Ensure that employees are clear on their roles and responsibilities:
  1. Know the job and their level of decision-making ability.
  2. Know the "game plan" for the work unit in terms of mission and objectives. These clearly stated goals will help to drive performance.
  3. Know how to measure the quality and output of results. The activities that are measured will get accomplished. This will also ensure that each activity has sufficient impact and is worth doing.
  4. Know the rewards and what they can expect in terms of recognition. This includes both monetary and non-monetary rewards.

5. Know where to get help when a problem occurs. These resources include the team leader, other team members and even resources outside the organization.

- Encourage peer coaching, in which each team member is available to give feedback and support to other team members on a regular basis.

Values Orientation

- When confronted with political or "turf" issues, ask yourself, "What actions/decisions are in the long-term best interest of the company?" Be willing to put aside or postpone personal interests if these conflict with broader company goals.
- Recognize that in the long run, opportunity and advancement usually go to those who demonstrate a commitment to broader company objectives. No one wins if the company doesn't win.
- Consider whether you are treating others (at all organizational levels) with the same respect with which you would like to be treated.
- If tempted or pressured to "short cut" regulatory or quality-assurance procedures, recognize the potential liabilities involved (both company and personal). Avoid actions/decisions with potential negative consequences that you would not want to live with.
- Consider whether your efforts to achieve personal career objectives are adversely affecting others. Recognize that if you do achieve your objectives, you will likely need the cooperation/commitment of the same individuals you are currently impacting.
- All work situations involve some degree of "politics." Be aware of and sensitive to political issues, but strive to be non-political in your dealings with others.
- Before making an important decision or taking an important action, ask yourself, "How would I respond if I owned the company?"
- Before you begin an assignment, identify the key players who are directly or indirectly involved. Include the appropriate individuals in the planning and decision-making loop.
- Deal with people honestly. Treat them with respect regardless of their position in the organization.

7

- Share information with appropriate individuals who would benefit by it. You never know when you are going to need information from someone else.
- Use staff meetings as a vehicle for encouraging cooperation and teamwork outside, as well as, within your work unit.
- Consider the people impacted by your work or decisions. Ask them for input and consider their perspective before developing your action plans.

Technical Expertise

- Prepare a position description which outlines the key responsibilities of your job.
- Identify the skills you need to successfully complete your job responsibilities.
- Assess your current skill level, and obtain feedback from your peers.
- Identify the sources available to increase your technical knowledge, including seminars, courses, reading material, etc.
- Identify a technical expert in your company who can serve as a mentor and coach to support your technical development.
- Look for opportunities to participate in professional organizations.
- Seek opportunities to make technical presentations as a guest speaker at technical conferences.

Examples of Basic Technical Skills and Industry Knowledge
1. Basic knowledge of fundamentals in primary area of work
2. Understanding of statistical methods for data analysis
3. Competency with computer applications and spreadsheets
4. Basic knowledge of technology in primary area of work
5. Knowledge of customer needs and product applications

Completing a Development Plan

Development plans serve to focus both an individual and his manager on a continuing program for the expansion of knowledge, skill and experience. The responsibility for the development plan rests with each individual. Companies may provide certain mechanisms and guidance, but the actual focus and discipline for advancing the plan comes from each individual's motivation and desire to learn more. Development plans may be oriented around both current and future jobs.

Review the **Development-Planning Worksheet** and use it as a guide to thinking through your own development plan. Who else in your work environment needs to be brought into your plan? How can you use this tool to assist other people in your work to set their own development plan into action?

Development-Planning Worksheet

NAME OF MANAGER

1. DEVELOPMENT GOAL

2. RESULTS TO BE ACHIEVED

3. DEVELOPMENT ACTIVITIES: TARGET DATE:

4. RESULTS REVIEWED (check one):
   _____ Bi-weekly
   _____ Monthly
   _____ Quarterly
   _____ Semi-annually
   _____ Other _____

5. DEVELOPMENT FOR:
   _____ Current Job (Job Title) _____
   _____ Future Job (Job Title) _____

Summary

Developing leadership ability is each person's responsibility in a self-directed leadership environment. There are many ways to go about this process. First, it is important to gain some accurate insight into one's own leadership competencies. Many tools and assessments are available to assist people with this awareness. Regardless of where one starts, there is great incentive based on the needs of companies both now and in the future to accept the responsibility for developing leadership capabilities. People mature along a leadership curve through the deliberate acquisition of leadership skills and knowledge over time and through practice and good coaching.

The leadership-development process includes a core set of competencies, an assessment of one's current abilities to be effective in using these competencies, a development plan and a means to assess progress and the initiative to revisit the plan on a periodic basis. Key leadership competencies have been identified in this chapter, and ways to obtain 360° feedback on one's capabilities, including insight to personal "blindspots," have been provided. There are numerous techniques you can implement to build your leadership competencies — this chapter provided over 100 of them.

Development plans are a key factor for guiding an individual's progress with enhancing their knowledge and skills in both current and future positions. Managers and employees act as partners in establishing development plans, but the major investment for guiding the course rests with the individual.

"The climax of leadership is to know when to do what."
John R. Scotford

7

210

Questions for Personal Development

1. What is the major emphasis of this chapter?

_____

_____

_____

_____

2. What are the most important things you learned from this chapter?

_____

_____

_____

_____

3. How can you apply what you learned to your current job?

_____

_____

_____

_____

4. How will you go about making these changes?

_____

_____

_____

_____

5. How can you monitor improvement?

_____

_____

_____

_____

6. Summarize the changes you expect to see in yourself one year from now.

_____

_____

_____

_____

7

211

*C*HAPTER 8

Next Generation of Leaders

What the Future Holds

Emerging trends in the global marketplace have a significant impact on the United States and the types of work and organizations that will exist in the future. As industry moves quickly toward the 21st century, many are heralding the explosions in technology that will continue to advance the *Information Age.*

Much like the Industrial Revolution of a century ago, the *Information Revolution* is having as significant an impact on work, jobs and lifestyles. And like the Industrial Revolution, this one cuts across all industries. The U.S. manufacturing base has been permanently eroded, with much of the work that used to be produced in this country relocated to other nations that are producing the same work in a more competitive way. Rather than debate the reality of this fact, the U.S. needs to aggressively frame its future in an equally powerful way. The nation needs to provide leadership and value to the world in pioneering the technologies and industries of the future.

More than ever, the U.S. needs a bold, creative and compelling leadership that will hold up a *vision,* set the direction and establish the *new* work requirements. These new work requirements will dictate the education and training needs of a nation, an industry and a company's people all along the way. Accepting or rejecting this leadership challenge will make the difference in who controls

> *"Be not afraid of greatness. Some are born great, some achieve greatness and some have greatness thrust upon them."*
> William Shakespeare

the destiny of a people. Given the leadership role of the United States, the impact is far reaching and long lasting.

As with any good *revolution* worth its name, the demand for leadership is pivotal to success in the future. Without a *vision, direction, goals* and a set of guiding *core values,* it is more difficult to establish *action plans* and create *work environments* that empower *individuals* to accelerate the agenda and, through unique and *reciprocal relationships,* make a difference. Reciprocity and partnering are pivotal factors in aligning motivation and assuring results harnessed to organizational and individual goals. The leadership roles presented in this book — those of **business leader, team leader and individual leader** — provide a frame of reference and an operational roadmap for unleashing the leader in everyone in the organization.

In any change cycle, resistance to change is always at a peak at the points of greatest impact — where change is imminent. The demands on leadership are keen to guide this revolution. Companies are dealing with the impact of these global trends on a daily basis. While the government must debate and shape the political destiny of a people, companies do not have time to "ponder." Companies must step up to bat quickly. They learned long ago "three strikes (or less) and you're out." Companies are experiencing fundamental change in all dimensions of work due to dramatic shifts in the world at large.

Many key factors are landing on the front doorstep of U.S. companies at the same time, including restructurings, downsizings, new product and process orientations and initiatives; new strategic-partnership models; global sourcing of capital (cash, labor and raw materials); rapid advances in communication and transportation; emerging and eager competitors; and shifts in lifestyles.

How do a country, an economy and a company go forward in an optimal and profitable way? How can the U.S. powerbase (e.g. research, education, invention, production, etc.) be reconfigured, revitalized and unleashed to become a totally new power in the world? How can companies and government work in collaboration to develop strategies to achieve goals?

8

> *"When you reach for the stars, you may not quite get one, but you won't come up with a handful of mud either."*
> Leo Burnett

These questions are significant because they are the ones your company must address — if not by working on them directly, then responding to their impact on a daily basis. The purpose of this chapter is to support your awareness of the larger issues your company is dealing with and how you can contribute both now and in the future. Whether you contribute at the division level, to your work group or team, or as an individual leader, you need to focus on the needs of the company in the future. You must determine what new skills you need to acquire to remain valuable to the goals of your company.

Developing Future Leaders

In developing future leaders, it is necessary to make projections about what leadership mindsets and capabilities will be useful to companies in the future. The paradigm shift in Chapter 6 demonstrates the change from *company- and control-driven to customer- and commitment-driven* work environments, where employees are empowered to lead. The main trend of the future is to make employees partners in the success of the company and to cultivate leadership in all positions.

The challenge exists to sort through the different types of leaders who will be required by companies in the future. Companies need to identify mindsets and capabilities, career-development experiences and *anticipated* leadership development and contributions which will be valued in the future. The following represents some of the shifts in leadership thinking and the *new* expectations for companies in the future. These shifts have an impact on developing leaders and shaping their roles as future contributors.

> *"We start with gifts. Merit comes from what we make of them."*
> Jean Toomer

8

215

8

Type of Leader

Leadership Expectations

Business Leader

Main Focus: To create a supportive environment and work culture for empowerment and to establish vision, live core values and set direction and broad goals for the company.

Past Experience: Broad-based and integrative; reflecting knowledge from several functional areas of the company as well as the industry in general. Exposures to technology, markets, business and different cultures. Effectiveness in leading/ inspiring people and business results.

Mindset and Capabilities: Entrepreneurial mindset — global thinking; customer- and commitment-driven; results-focused; leader/collaborator and follower; flexibility; synthesizer, simplifier, communicator; mentor, innovator, energizer, revitalizer; strategic opportunist; flexible, adaptable, embracer of differences; curious; ongoing learner for leveraging industry, market and lifestyle trends to company advantage.

Training, Development and Contribution: Multi-skill development with progressive technical development in step with major career focus, e.g., marketing, finance, law, information systems, organization development/human resources. Early career-training points include orientation and integration experiences to stimulate functional excellence and then a leveraging of company capabilities. Mid-career assignments and development are broadening and rely less on technical knowledge and more on strengthening entrepreneurial, cross-cultural and business savvy. Later career development is centered on leveraging all knowledge and experience to optimize company capability. This may include contributions to totally unfamiliar functions or businesses depending on the strength of the individual leader to inspire others to translate *principles of generalship* into useful applications for their part of the industry.

Team Leader   *Main Focus:* To deploy the leadership initiative and nurture self-directed leadership among team members; create action plans in sync with company and business goals.

Past Experience: Functional and/or technical responsibilities with demonstrated effectiveness, interpersonal communication and relationship skills.

Mindset and Capabilities: Connector, promoter, developer; customer- and commitment-driven; action-focused; environmental scanner, synthesizer and improver; facilitator, coach, influencer, resource; stimulator, simplifier, integrator, expeditor; leader/follower and collaborator; flexibility; leverager and harmonizer of differences; communicator, translator, mediator; enabler, enforcer, applauder.

Training, Development and Contribution: Early career and training experiences may be of a technical and/or functional nature or based on team management and development skills. Early training also may be focused on psychology and human development centered on motivation, productivity and fulfillment at work and in the adult life cycle. Mid-career developmental steps needed to broaden the individual to include expanded knowledge about the industry, company and competitor operations and an area of specific expertise. Product and process-development knowledge is key in responding competitively to market trends. Rapid assimilation of new techniques and improvement methods is an advantage in developing others to do the same. Later career assignments can benefit from progressive responsibility in the management of teams and processes with focused business results.

8

Individual Leader

Main Focus: To leverage abilities to meet individual and team goals, to achieve business results (established in individual and team action plans that link to company goals) and to become effective in self-directed leadership that propels the team and the company forward through new ideas and processes.

Past Experience: Technical and/or functional assignments as individual contributor on other teams and/or as a team leader who now is a member on another team. Proficiency in team-member and self-directed leadership skills maturing in step with increased opportunity and exposures.

Mindset and Capabilities: Contributor, discoverer; customer- and commitment driven; follower/leader and collaborator flexibility; processor, synthesizer, leverager/optimizer, improver; resourcer, synthesizer, communicator; implementer, initiator, integrator.

Training, Development and Contribution: Early training aligns with areas of specific technical and/or functional expertise with a focus on accelerated performance in high-commitment, self-directed leadership environments. Mid-career assignments and development include more depth in an area of specialty and increased opportunities to work in teams with increasingly difficult performance expectations in more complex team work assignments. Cross-cultural and cross-divisional experiences are highly valued in readying individuals to perform well as members of global teams. Some individual leaders are naturals for evolving both early in their careers and at mid- or later points. Some individual leaders opt to remain focused in areas of specialty (medical or very technical fields for instance) and become "expert" individual leaders in their career progression. Later career experiences take advantage of team-member and team-leader behavior in ever more challenging settings, including mentoring the development of other individual leaders and/or team leaders.

Redefining the Practice of Leadership

The key challenge companies face in empowering their workforce is to redefine the practice of leadership. The beginning contrast in this book between management and leadership presented management as *doing things right* and leadership as *doing the right things*. The premise of self-directed leadership is that people throughout the organization should be trained, developed, coached, mentored, recognized and rewarded along the way for initiating and contributing in unique ways to the business success of the company.

Here is one way to frame leadership as is intended in high-commitment, self-directed leadership environments:

Leadership is present in all employees and positions throughout the company. The authority to act accompanies the scope of work and responsibility that individuals have in their daily work. Each individual understands his or her link and contribution to the "big picture." Yet, the vision, goals, core values and work environment is clear and empowered enough to bring focus and reality to action plans and the attainment of business results.

Leadership is both self-motivated and company-empowered where individuals are expected to contribute their ideas for improving performance throughout the company in such areas as:

- customer satisfaction
- product integrity and development
- quality and innovation
- work-process flows
- market knowledge
- research and innovation

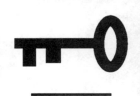

Self-directed leadership brings out the highest potential of each individual and supports his or her initiations and innovations. The new company contributors understand their value in terms of their flexibility and adaptability to new industry and marketplace demands. They are motivated by partnering with their companies to develop their technical expertise as well as their interpersonal abilities to influence and collaborate with others. Leadership in the 21st century is in everyone's role since the responsibility for the future is one that must be shared and one that requires reciprocal

Self-Directed Leadership Paradigm Shift

From	*To*
Manager mindset and skills	Leadership mindset and skills
Boss	Coach, mentor, collaborator
Control, centralized authority	Empowerment, commitment and distributed authority
Short-term, narrow focus	Long-term, broad vision
Short leash	Independence
Internal competition	Global realities
Forced change and compliance	Entrepreneurism, innovation
Rules and regulations	Shared values and cultural norms
Position power, hierarchy	Relationship power, networks
Departments, work groups	Teams
Blaming, isolating	Collaborating, unifying
Schedules, numbers	Quality and service
Inward, product-driven	Outward, customer-driven

Examining Your Own Outlook on Leadership

To meet the increased challenge of today's and tomorrow's companies, our view and practice of leadership needs to redefine itself in terms of the **AIM Leadership Model — Action, Influence and Motivation.** Self-directed leadership requires self-examination of one's own values related to responsibility, professional development and desired work environment. Review the following questions and your responses to organize your current thinking. How prepared are you to be a leader in the companies and work cultures of the next century?

AIM Leadership Model

ACTION — Vision, Core Values and Change

1. Have I worked on a team or in a company that wants my ideas? Am I expected to be a leader now? Do I like these expectations?
2. Have I worked for an organization that "walks the talk" — practices its core values? Have I ever worked in an environment that does not? What difference does it make? How will it influence my next move?
3. How comfortable am I with change? What changes have I made in the last one to three years as a result of company change? How is it going?
4. Next time, do I want to be out in front of the change? How can I make that happen? What new or expanded skills do I need to become more effective in self-directed leadership?

INFLUENCE — Perception, Relationships and Utilization

1. What success have I had in clarifying my observations and perceptions with others in my company? Have I found mentors and coaches that bring wisdom and reflection to the process?
2. Do I believe the leadership practices at my company are deliberate or haphazard? Do the company's communication methods improve or hinder my perceptions of "what is really going on" at the company?
3. Am I bringing out the best in others by valuing and respecting differences and by collaborating in purposeful ways? Do I seek the same from others? Where are the breakdowns? Now what?

8

by collaborating in purposeful ways? Do I seek the same from others?
Where are the breakdowns? Now what?

4. Have I mastered a way to gauge when and how to influence my boss, peers
   and those whose work I may direct? Who in my company provides a good
   role model for coaching and influencing? Are they respected, recognized
   and rewarded for this behavior? How can I expand my influencing skills?

MOTIVATION — Understanding Needs, Feedback and Performance

1. How am I balancing the need for achieving results with the need to work
   with others? How can I commit to balancing my personal and professional
   life?

2. How am I sharing responsibility and recognition at work? Am I a
   developmental and motivational leader/contributor inspiring others and
   being inspired on a daily basis?

3. Do I ask others what they need from me at work? Do I tell others what I
   need from them? How do people in my work group give positive and
   negative feedback to one another? Are there gaps here that need to be
   adjusted? How so?

4. How am I and how is my team using motivation to influence performance?

How can I leverage my motivation to spark increased motivation in others?

Summary

In order to work effectively in the companies of the future, individuals and companies will partner in accepting the leadership challenge. They will do whatever is necessary to learn new processes and create systems that support optimal productivity in a very competitive marketplace.

Individuals and companies must become skillful at easily shifting from leader to follower and follower to collaborator. Commitments to share information quickly and develop people more efficiently in essential skills will strengthen a company as it seeks to empower its people and gain responsive contributions. Individuals will commit readily to continuous learning and be challenged by rising to the occasion of taking on new responsibilities.

Self-directed leadership requires that individuals and companies build a motivational and developmental work culture. Learning what one doesn't know will light new fires even under a company's most expert member of the "brain trust." Key achievements will include innovations in product and process design, inventions and deployment of leapfrog technologies and ever more deliberate ways of serving customers. Catering to niche markets anywhere in the world will also be the cornerstones of 21st-century companies and the people who make them work. The principles and practices guided by the **AIM Leadership Model — Action, Influence and Motivation** — begin your leadership journey into the next century. It is a journey you will want to assess deliberately and routinely. One principle is certain: Change is a constant, and if you don't want to be left behind, get out in front and lead.

> *"The whole secret of a successful life is to find out what it is one's destiny to do, and then do it."*
> Henry Ford

8

223

Questions for Personal Development

1. What is the major emphasis of this chapter?

_____

_____

_____

_____

2. What are the most important things you learned from this chapter?

_____

_____

_____

_____

3. How can you apply what you learned to your current job?

_____

_____

_____

_____

4. How will you go about making these changes?

_____

_____

_____

_____

5. How can you monitor improvement?

_____

_____

_____

_____

6. Summarize the changes you expect to see in yourself one year from now.

_____

_____

_____

_____

Resources

Bennis, Warren and Bert Nanus. *Leaders: The Strategies for Taking Charge.* New York, Harper and Row, 1985.

Bothwell, Lin. *The Art of Leadership.* New York, Prentice Hall, 1983.

Cohen, Allan and David Bradford. *Influence Without Authority.* New York, John Wiley and Sons, 1991.

DiLenschneider, Robert L. *A Briefing for Leaders: Communication as the Ultimate Exercise of Power.* New York, Harper Business, 1992.

Frohman, Alan L. and Leonard W. Johnson. *Middle Management Challenge: Moving From Crisis to Empowerment.* New York, McGraw-Hill, 1992.

Hersey, Paul D. *The Situational Leader.* Warner Books, New York, 1984.

Hickman, Craig. *Mind of a Manager, Soul of a Leader.* New York, John Wiley and Sons, 1991.

Kotter, John P. *A Force for Change: How Leadership Differs From Management.* New York, Free Press, 1990.

Kotter, John P. *Power and Influence Beyond Formal Authority.* New York, Free Press, 1985.

Kouzes, James and Barry Posner. *Credibility: How Leaders Can Gain and Lose It, Why People Demand It.* San Francisco, Jossey-Bass, 1993.

Maxwell, John C. *Developing the Leader in You.* Nashville, Thomas Nelson Publishers, 1993.

McNeil, Art. *"I" of the Hurricane: Creating Corporate Energy.* Toronto, Stoddart Publishers, 1987.

Nanus, Bert. *The Leader's Edge.* Contemporary Books, Chicago, 1989.

Tichey, Noel M. and Mary Anne Devanna. *The Transformational Leader.* New York, John Wiley and Sons, 1990.

Tichey, Noel M. and Straford Sherman. *Control Your Destiny or Someone Else Will.* New York, DoubleDay, 1993.

Weisbord, Marvin R. *Productive Workplaces.* San Francisco, Jossey-Bass, 1987.

INDEX